TURNING THE
WORLD
⬆UPSIDE DOWN⬇

TURNING THE
WORLD
↑UPSIDE DOW↓N

A DEVOTIONAL COMMENTARY ON ACTS

Huw Rees, Iain Maclean & Jeremy Gibson

RITCHIE

John Ritchie Publishing

40 Beansburn, Kilmarnock, Scotland

ISBN-13: 978 1 914273 51 3

Copyright © 2024 by John Ritchie Ltd.
40 Beansburn, Kilmarnock, Scotland

www.ritchiechristianmedia.co.uk

Typeset by John Ritchie Ltd., Kilmarnock
Printed by Short Run Press, Exeter

Jeremy Gibson wrote the general introduction, the introductions to Parts 2 and 3, and Paul's third missionary journey (17), chapters 2-4, 9, 12, 14, 16, 18, and 20, and co-authored chapters 7 and 11 with Huw Rees who also wrote chapters 5, 6, 8, and 21-23. Iain Maclean wrote the introduction to the second missionary journey (13) and chapters 1, 10, 15, 19, and 24.

Graphics by Stewart Rollo.

ABBREVIATIONS

AD   Anno Domini

BC   Before Christ

ESV   English Standard Version

JND   New Translation by J.N. Darby 1939

NASB   New American Standard Bible

NKJV   New King James Version

YLT   Young's Literal Translation

CONTENTS

INTRODUCTION

The Acts of the Apostles is Luke's beautifully crafted companion to his Gospel. Written with artistic finesse, historical accuracy, and spiritual perception, it documents the birth of the church and the rapid dissemination of the gospel message throughout the first century Mediterranean world. The absence of any mention of the rampant persecution of Christians which raged following the great fire of Rome in AD 64 and the destruction of the Jerusalem temple in AD 70 suggests that Luke completed it shortly after Paul's first Roman imprisonment of AD 59-61.

With irresistible power, the church grew, and the gospel spread far and wide, transforming lives, saving souls, and cutting across every kind of class and cultural divide. Energised by the Holy Spirit, the apostles and their associates fearlessly witnessed to Christ's resurrection 'in Jerusalem, and in all Judaea, and in Samaria, and unto the uttermost part of the earth' (1.8). The universal use of the Greek language, the political stability and efficient transport links of the Roman Empire all facilitated this movement of the gospel. Paul, as an insightful strategist and Roman citizen, realised that if he established churches at key communication centres, he could reach more people with the gospel faster. As the believers 'went forth, and preached everywhere, the Lord [worked] with *them* … confirming the word with signs following' (Mk 16.20). He kept adding 'to the church daily such as should be saved' (2.47; cf. 5.14; 6.1; 9.31; 11.21, 24; 16.5) with the result that 'the word of God grew and multiplied' (12.24; cf. 6.7).

Acts covers a period of approximately 30 years (c AD 30-61). Roughly speaking, chapters 1-12 describe the first half and chapters 13-28 the second half. Chapters 1-7 focus on Peter's service at Jerusalem; apart from the fifty days before Pentecost (2.1), a couple of consecutive days (4.5; 5.21) and one three-hour period (5.7), they contain no time indicators. Chapters 13-28 cover Paul's wider ministry, including the ten years he travelled almost 10,000 miles during three missionary journeys,[1] two years imprisonment in Caesarea (24.27), and two in Rome (28.30). In this section, Luke's references to historical events and characters allow us to anchor the text within a more definitive timeframe. For example, the Emperor Claudius expelled the Jews from Rome about AD 49/ 50 (18.2),[2] Gallio became the proconsul of Achaia in July AD 51 (18.12)[3] and Porcius Festus was appointed in AD 59 (24.27).[4]

While chapters 1-7 and 13-28 follow a linear chronology, chapters 8 to 12 do not. At times they record overlapping events to show how Stephen's stoning triggered a shift in attention from Jerusalem to Samaria and to the uttermost parts of the earth, from Jews to Gentiles and from Peter to Paul. Persecuted believers, who were scattered throughout Judaea, Samaria, Phenice, Cyprus and Antioch, 'went every where preaching the word' (8.1, 4; 11.19). Philip himself preached Christ to the city of Samaria (8.5) and when the apostles, who remained 'at Jerusalem heard that Samaria had received the word of God, they sent unto them Peter and John' (8.14). Returning to Jerusalem, they 'preached the gospel in many villages of the Samaritans' (8.25).

Meanwhile, Saul, who had assented to Stephen's stoning, was dramatically converted at Damascus (8.1; 9.1-8). Afterwards, Saul spent three years in Arabia before returning to Damascus and then visiting Jerusalem, where Barnabas introduced him to the church, and he stayed with Peter for fifteen days (9.20-29; 22.17-21; Gal

1.18). When his life was threatened, Saul escaped from Jerusalem to Tarsus, where he spent 'the best part of ten unchronicled years'[5] (9.30). It was probably during this time that he established the churches of Cilicia, which he later revisited and strengthened in the company of Silas (15.41). Since Saul hailed from Tarsus, we learn from his example the importance of witnessing at home (9.11; 21.39; 22.3; cf. Mk 5.19).

The conversion of Cornelius was a key turning point which was designed to convince Jewish believers that God had 'to the Gentiles granted repentance unto life' (9.32-11.18). Convinced of this, when the Jerusalem church heard that many in Antioch had 'turned unto the Lord', they sent Barnabas to that city (11.19-24). He retrieved Saul from Tarsus and together they taught the Antioch church for one year (11.25, 26). When Agabus prophesied at Antioch about an imminent famine, in an act of great generosity, this Gentile church sent a gift by Saul and Barnabas to the Jerusalem church (11.27-30). Having delivered the gift, they returned to Antioch with John Mark (12.25). It was about this time (AD 44) that James was executed, and an angel delivered Peter from prison before smiting Herod Agrippa (12.1-23).[6]

Acts is a book about people, how they interact with each other and how they surprise us. Who would have imagined that Barnabas, a generous and kindly believer (4.36, 37), would eventually partner with Saul of Tarsus, originally an intense and violent persecutor of the church (8.1; 9.1-8)? And who, seeing them working so closely together at Antioch (11.25, 26), labouring harmoniously throughout a whole missionary journey (13, 14) and jointly attending the Jerusalem Council (15.1, 2), would have foreseen their eventual split (15.37-39)? John Mark, who left them during their first missionary journey, was the cause of the contention (13.13). But we should never write anyone off. Barnabas' nephew proved good.

He served with Barnabas at Cyprus (15.39), was fondly regarded by the Apostle Peter (1 Pet 5.13), and even visited Paul during his first Roman imprisonment (Col 4.10). John Mark's written legacy is a Gospel about the perfect, unfailing Servant.

No one, not even the Apostle Paul, can achieve anything without others. Having completed his first missionary journey with Barnabas, he started his second with Silas (15.40, 41). Timothy joined them at Derbe and Lystra (16.1-3). Luke, who indicated his personal involvement in the story with the pronoun 'we', joined them at Troas but then remained at Philippi while they went on (16.8-10; 17.1). It was here, at Philippi, that he re-joined Paul during his third missionary journey (20.6). After that, they were practically inseparable. Luke stayed with Paul till his arrest at Jerusalem (21.15, 33). He then re-joined Paul at Caesarea, travelling with him all the way to Rome (27.1; 28.16). During Paul's second Roman incarceration, he wrote to Timothy, 'Only Luke is with me' (2 Tim 4.11). What an unexpected, yet fruitful friendship! Between them, 'an Hebrew of the Hebrews' and a Gentile physician, they wrote more than half the New Testament (Phil 3.5).

Others helped Paul. Together, they teach us that our service is carefully choreographed by God to ensure it works hand in hand with that of others (cf. Eph 2.10), and that we should be willing to serve in one place for a long time, or move, as the Lord directs (cf. Num 9.15-23). At Corinth, Paul stayed with Aquila and Priscilla, who travelled with him to Ephesus, where they, in turn, encouraged Apollos (18.1-3, 18, 19, 24-27). During Paul's third missionary journey 'there accompanied him into Asia Sopater of Berea; and of the Thessalonians, Aristarchus and Secundus; and Gaius of Derbe, and Timotheus; and of Asia, Tychicus and Trophimus' (20.4). Sopater was with Paul during his three-month stay in Greece when he wrote the Roman epistle (20.1-3; Rom 16.21). Aristarchus had been with him at Ephesus and went on to travel with him to Rome, where he was a fellow prisoner (19.29; 27.2; Col 4.10). Tychicus was 'a beloved brother, and a faithful minister and fellowservant in the Lord', who carried Paul's letters to Ephesus and Colosse (Eph 6.21; Col 4.7, 8). He remained true right up to Paul's execution at Rome (2 Tim 4.12; Titus 3.12). After many years of faithful service, Trophimus succumbed to illness at Miletus (2 Tim 4.20). Some twenty years after Philip the evangelist spoke to the Ethiopian eunuch, Paul stayed with Philip at Caesarea, where he had settled and raised four godly daughters (8.40; 21.8, 9). It was here that Agabus prophesied yet again, this time concerning Paul's imprisonment (21.10, 11).

Alas, this book, which charts so carefully the beginning of the church era, has generated much controversy and discord. Some teach that Acts, in all its details, is a precise blueprint for church practice today. The regular conversion of thousands is the expected norm (2.41; 4.4). Speaking in tongues is needed to evidence salvation (2.4; 10.46; 19.6). Supernatural healings (including raising the dead), demonic exorcisms, and prophecies should continue (3.6-8; 5.12-16; 9.32-41; 11.28; 14.8-10; 16.16-18; 19.11, 12; 20.9-12; 21.10; 28.7-10). And, once saved, there is an invariable delay till a second blessing when the Holy Spirit is received through the laying on of the hands of apostles (8.14-18; 19.1-6). People crave this kind of Pentecostal-style revival and actively attempt to manufacture it. A dangerous thing to do!

One problem with this interpretation of Acts is that it runs contrary to the teaching of the New Testament letters. At the end of Paul's life, he noticed widespread declension, not exponential expansion. In his final letter, he wrote, 'This thou knowest, that all they which are in Asia be turned away from me ... This know also, that in the last days perilous times shall come. For men shall be lovers of their own selves ... Having a form of godliness, but denying the power thereof' (2 Tim 1.15; 3.1, 5). Peter warned that 'there shall be false teachers among you, who privily shall bring in damnable heresies, even denying the Lord that bought them, and bring upon themselves swift destruction. And many shall follow their pernicious ways; by reason of whom the way of truth shall be evil spoken of' (2 Pet 2.1, 2). Jude alerted his readers that 'there are certain men crept in unawares, who were before of old ordained to this condemnation, ungodly men, turning the grace of our God into lasciviousness, and denying the only Lord God, and our Lord Jesus Christ' (Jude 4).

The present fascination with so-called tongues speaking flies in the face of Paul's clear instructions to the Corinthians. He emphasised that spiritual gifts should be exercised in church gatherings with the loving intention of mutual edification; and, for this to be achieved, all vocal participation needed to be understood (1 Cor 13.1; 14.1-5). Quoting Isaiah, Paul wrote, 'In the law it is written, With *men of* other tongues and other lips will I speak unto this people; and yet for all that will they not hear me, saith the Lord. Wherefore tongues are for a sign, not to them that believe, but to them that believe not' (1 Cor 14.21, 22). That is to say, tongues were primarily intended to challenge unbelievers (especially Jewish ones), not build up Christians. Moreover, that function was temporary: 'whether *there be* tongues, they shall cease' (1 Cor 13.8). The epistles repeatedly emphasise that Christians should fix their focus on the spiritual, not the physical, the eternal, not the temporal, the heavenly, not the earthly. Paul blessed 'the God and Father of our Lord Jesus Christ, who hath blessed us with all spiritual blessings in heavenly *places* in Christ' (Eph 1.3). As he wrote to the Corinthians, 'we look not at the things which are seen, but at the things which are not seen: for the things which are seen *are* temporal; but the things which are not seen *are* eternal' (2 Cor 4.18). From his Roman prison, Paul exhorted the Colossians, 'Set your affection on things above, not on things on the earth' (Col 3.2). When professing Christians push a health and wealth gospel, with the expectation of perfect physical health and material prosperity right now, they are prioritising the wrong things at the wrong time. God will indeed give us a perfect body free from sin and illness, but not till the Lord's coming (Phil 3.21). At the moment, 'the whole creation groaneth and travaileth in pain together until now. And not only *they*, but ourselves also, which have the firstfruits of the Spirit, even we ourselves groan within ourselves, waiting for the adoption, *to wit*, the redemption of our body' (Rom 8.22, 23). The suggestion that Christians look for a second blessing of the Spirit contradicts Paul's affirmation that 'if any man have not the Spirit of Christ, he is none of his' (Rom 8.9). In other words, the Holy Spirit is now received in all His fullness as soon as an individual is born again. The notion that there are apostles today is also preposterous. The church is 'built upon the foundation of the apostles and prophets, Jesus Christ himself being the chief corner *stone*' (Eph 2.20). That foundation layer was established in the first century and can never be re-laid.

A second flaw with the assumption that everything in Acts applies today is the failure to appreciate its transitional character. For example, the preaching in the first few chapters seems to have held out the very real possibility that, had Israel repented and believed, Christ's millennial kingdom would have been ushered in immediately. Peter declared, 'Repent ye therefore, and be converted, that your sins may be blotted out, when the times of refreshing shall come from the presence of the Lord; And he shall send Jesus Christ, which before was preached unto you: Whom the heaven must receive until the times of restitution of all things, which God hath spoken by the mouth of all his holy prophets since the world began' (3.19-21). As well as demonstrating God's kindness to suffering humanity, validating of the apostolic message (Heb 2.3, 4), and furnishing proof that Christ had truly risen from the dead (4.10), the early healing miracles anticipated the widespread health to be enjoyed by the citizens of Messiah's glorious kingdom (cf. Isa 35.5, 6). This offer of the kingdom ended with the stoning of Stephen.

The birth of the church on the Day of Pentecost also marked a radical shift in God's dealings with men. The longstanding hostility between Jews and Gentiles was broken down. Through His cross, Christ 'made both one, and hath broken down the middle wall of partition *between [Jews and Gentiles]*' (Eph 2.14). But clarity was needed as to how Gentiles (and saved Jews) stood in relation to the Law of Moses. And how would these ancient ethnic divisions between Jews, Samaritans and Gentiles be broken down in practical terms? In Acts there are four distinct episodes where believers either spoke with tongues or there appeared to be a delay in their receiving the Holy Spirit after they believed. Three of these four events related either to the birth of the church or the dissolution of these national barriers. First, at Pentecost, unbelieving Jews and Gentile proselytes were amazed when the Galilean disciples, filled with the Holy Spirit, spoke in their own languages 'the wonderful works of God' (2.4-11). Second, the Samaritans, who 'received the word of God', only received the Holy Ghost after Peter and John laid '*their* hands on them' (8.14, 17). Although it is not specifically mentioned that they spoke with tongues, there must have been a visible manifestation that they had received the Spirit. Why the delay, at this time, between believing God's word and receiving the Spirit? Historically, the Jews had 'no dealings with the Samaritans' (Jn 4.9). This state of affairs could not continue in the Christian church. How better to rectify this schism than if they received the

Holy Spirit by the laying on of the hands of two Jewish apostles who had come from Jerusalem to Samaria? Thirdly, as soon as Cornelius and his friends believed the gospel, they too spoke with tongues, convincing Peter and his Jewish companions that these Gentiles had truly received the Holy Spirit (10.44-48).

The fourth occurrence was at Ephesus, where Paul discovered twelve disciples who were living in a kind of dispensational time-warp, following the incomplete preaching of Apollos (19.1-7). They had neither heard of, nor received the Holy Spirit. Instead of undergoing Christian baptism, they had been baptised unto John's 'baptism of repentance' (19.4). As soon as Paul explained the anticipatory nature of John's message, which challenged his hearers to 'believe on him which should come after him, that is, on Christ Jesus', they believed the truth and were 'baptized in the name of the Lord Jesus' (19.4, 5). Their position was unique, as was their reception of the Spirit, mediated through the laying on of Paul's hands and confirmed by their speaking foreign languages and prophesying (19.6). None of these events established standard church practice. Instead, they were dealing with specific issues that needed to be addressed in the early experience of the church.

The principles which Acts establishes for current church practice and Christian mission must be practically workable, consistent with the teaching of the epistles, and take into account the transitional nature of the book. At Pentecost, 'they that gladly received [Peter's] word were baptized' (2.41). The Lord Jesus commissioned His followers to make disciples of 'all nations, baptizing them in the name of the Father, and of the Son, and of the Holy Ghost' (Mt 28.19). Throughout Acts, everyone who professed faith in Christ was, without delay, baptised by immersion (8.12, 13, 16, 36, 38; 9.18; 10.47, 48; 11.16; 16.15, 33; 18.8; 19.3-5; 22.16). This remains the pattern for today.

Those who believed 'continued stedfastly in the apostles' doctrine and fellowship, and in breaking of bread, and in prayers' (2.42). The apostles placed such an emphasis on Bible teaching that they appointed others to deal with the physical needs of the saints, while they gave themselves 'continually to prayer, and to the ministry of the word' (6.6). Today, any local church which neglects the teaching of God's word will eventually flounder. Just as the early believers remembered the Lord Jesus by breaking bread on the first day of each week, local churches should continue this weekly practice (cf. 20.7). Luke repeatedly emphasised the importance of personal and corporate prayer (1.13, 14; 4.23-31; 6.4-6; 9.11, 40; 10.9; 12.5, 12; 13.3; 14.23; 16.25; 20.36; 21.5; 22.17; 28.8). These truths continue to be vitally important to the life of every Christian and local church. No prayer, no power. It was when they 'that believed were of one heart and of one soul … with great power gave the apostles witness of the resurrection of the Lord Jesus' (4.32, 33). Loving care for fellow believers remains the bedrock for effective Christian witness. As the Saviour said, 'By this shall all *men* know that ye are my disciples, if ye have love one to another' (Jn 13.35).

As Luke's narrative unfolds, the gospel moved out by public preaching and personal evangelism, each energised and directed by the Holy Spirit. Peter preached to crowds in the Jerusalem temple (2.14-40; 3.12-26) and, with the other apostles and Stephen, witnessed to the Jewish Sanhedrin (4.8-12; 5.29-32; 7.1-60). Philip conversed with an Ethiopian eunuch (8.30-35) and Peter spoke to Cornelius and his Gentile friends (10.34-43). During his missionary journeys, Paul taught in Jewish synagogues (13.16-41; 17.2, 3), forbad a Gentile from worshipping him (14.15-18), and disputed with Athenian philosophers (17.22-31). Arrested at Jerusalem, Paul bore testimony before a Jewish mob (21.40-22.21) and stirred discord among the Jewish leaders (23.6). At Caesarea, he defended himself before the Jews and Felix (24.10-21), spoke privately to Felix and his wife Drusilla (24.24, 25), defended himself yet again before his Jewish detractors and Porcius Festus (25.8), and gave his testimony before King Agrippa, Bernice, and Festus (26.1-23). Having witnessed to the Jews at Rome (28.23-29), Paul continued 'preaching the kingdom of God, and teaching those things which concern the Lord Jesus Christ, with all confidence, no man forbidding him' (28.31).

While the style of preaching varied depending on who was preaching, and to whom, the fundamentals remained the same. Every sermon was thoroughly biblical, either quoting from or alluding to Old Testament scripture, or resting upon the great doctrines of God. Christ was at the heart of everything that was said, especially the historical facts and enormous spiritual ramifications of His death and resurrection. He is the only Saviour (4.12), Who has been exalted and will return as this world's future Judge (10.42; 17.31). With great courage, the believers preached this gospel, first to the Jews and then to the Gentiles (4.20; 9.27; 11.19; cf. Rom 1.16), calling on their audiences to repent and receive remission of sins and the gift of the Holy Spirit.

This is the same message we preach today. And it has the same results. In the Acts, some believed, many were indifferent or negative, and some turned violent (cf. 2.41; 4.1-22; 5.17-40; 8.1, 3; 9.1, 2; 14.1, 2, 19; 17.1-5; 18.12, 13; 21.27-31; 28.23, 24). Most persecution came from the Jews. Even when Herod Agrippa killed James and imprisoned Peter, he was encouraged to do so because it pleased the Jews (12.1-3). Gentiles opposed Paul at Philippi and Ephesus because the transforming power of the gospel affected their income (16.19; 19.24-27). At Ephesus, the aggression was so severe that Paul wrote to the Corinthians, 'I have fought with beasts at Ephesus' (15.32). But persecution did not hinder the gospel; rather, it accelerated its spread.

Sadly, the church's greatest threat was from within, not without. Pride, deception, and division quickly raised their ugly heads. Craving esteem, Ananias and Sapphira faked generosity, for which they were judged (4.32-5.11). Dissatisfaction with the distribution of funds provoked unrest among believers (6.1). Even Paul and Barnabas eventually split (15.39). If history has taught us anything, the enemy within remains the biggest threat to the church. We should pray that God will help us maintain harmony in local churches and reach out with fervour to the masses with this powerful, life-changing gospel. If we do this, we will fulfil Christ's purpose for His church: 'ye shall be witnesses unto me both in Jerusalem, and in all Judaea, and in Samaria, and unto the uttermost part of the earth' (1.8).

Greek words used more often in Acts than any other NT book

Word	Times used	Word	Times used
Pneuma (refers to Holy Spirit in all but x17)	70	Homothumadon (one accord)	11
		Anastasis (resurrection)	11
'Jerusalem'	60	Proseuchē (prayer)	9
Apostolos (apostle)	30	Proskartereō (continue)	6
Marturus (witness)	13		

Paul's letters

Letter	Place and time of writing
1 and 2 Thessalonians	During eighteen-month stay at Corinth (18.5, 11)
1 Corinthians	During two-year and three-month stay at Ephesus (19.8, 10)
2 Corinthians	In Macedonia (20.1, 2)
Romans	During three-month stay in Greece (20.2, 3)
Ephesians, Philippians, Colossians and Philemon	During first Roman imprisonment (28.30, 31; Eph 3.1; 4.1; 6.20; Phil 1.7, 13; Col 4.3, 18; Philem 10, 13, 22)
1 Timothy and Titus	After first Roman imprisonment
2 Timothy	Awaiting execution, during second Roman imprisonment
Galatians	Perhaps during second or third missionary journey

CHRONOLOGY OF THE ACTS OF THE APOSTLES

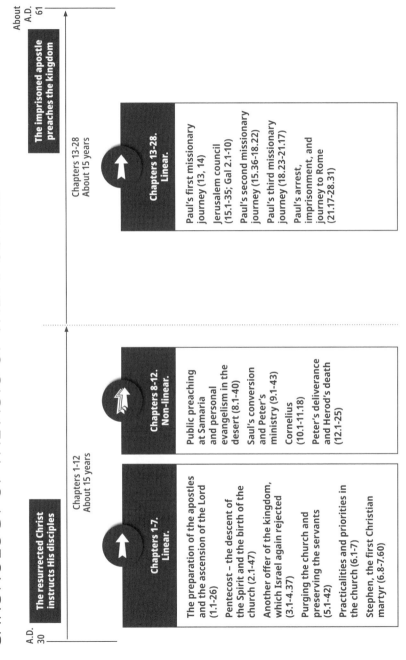

A.D. 30

The resurrected Christ instructs His disciples

Chapters 1-12
About 15 years

Chapters 1-7. Linear.

The preparation of the apostles and the ascension of the Lord (1.1-26)

Pentecost – the descent of the Spirit and the birth of the church (2.1-47)

Another offer of the kingdom, which Israel again rejected (3.1-4.37)

Purging the church and preserving the servants (5.1-42)

Practicalities and priorities in the church (6.1-7)

Stephen, the first Christian martyr (6.8-7.60)

Chapters 8-12. Non-linear.

Public preaching at Samaria and personal evangelism in the desert (8.1-40)

Saul's conversion and Peter's ministry (9.1-43)

Cornelius (10.1-11.18)

Peter's deliverance and Herod's death (12.1-25)

The imprisoned apostle preaches the kingdom

Chapters 13-28
About 15 years

Chapters 13-28. Linear.

Paul's first missionary journey (13, 14)

Jerusalem council (15.1-35; Gal 2.1-10)

Paul's second missionary journey (15.36-18.22)

Paul's third missionary journey (18.23-21.17)

Paul's arrest, imprisonment, and journey to Rome (21.17-28.31)

About A.D. 61

PART 1

JERUSALEM, JUDAEA, AND SAMARIA
(1.1-8.25)

1

THE PREPARATION OF THE APOSTLES AND THE ASCENSION OF THE LORD (1.1-26)

WHILE THE GOSPELS RECORD the beginning on earth of the Lord Jesus' great work of salvation (Heb 2.3), Acts records its continuation through His apostles, who were empowered from heaven by the Holy Spirit. Redemption was gloriously accomplished when Christ cried 'finished' (Jn 19.30), but the risen Lord is presently engaged in the ongoing work of applying that redemption: sinners are still being saved and saints sustained (Heb 7.25).

Luke wrote his Gospel and the Acts to establish his friend, Theophilus, in essential Christian doctrine. Theophilus was probably an official in the Roman empire because, like Felix (23.26) and Festus (26.25), he is introduced as 'most excellent' (Lk 1.3). The gospel is needed by, offered to, and sufficient for all levels in society (1 Tim 2.1-4). Theophilus' name means 'friend of God', a relationship the Lord encouraged: 'ye are my friends, if ye do whatsoever I command you' (Jn 15.14).

Preparation (vv3-8)

The apostles entered the 40-day period between the resurrection and the ascension *sad* that their hopes for a national deliverer had been dashed (Lk 24.27,21) and *sceptical* of the initial resurrection reports (Lk 24.11). Peter was *surprised* to find the tomb empty, and the two whom the Lord spoke to on the road to Emmaus were *slow* to believe the scriptures which foretold Messiah's suffering (Lk 24.25). But not long into that 40-day period they became sure He had risen. To accomplish this **vital transformation** the risen Lord used 'many sure proofs' (1.3, Weymouth), showing Himself alive, not to one person alone - leaving no possible corroboration - but to twelve official witnesses and to many unofficial witnesses (1 Cor 15.6).

On these occasions a wide range of **spoken interactions** occurred between the risen Lord and the twelve. There was *exposition*, for the Lord spoke 'of the things pertaining to the kingdom of God' (1.3). This included laying out the scriptural expectation of His resurrection (Lk 24.25-27), which put it on a 'more sure' footing than even eyewitness testimony (2 Pet 1.19). Further, there was the opportunity for a *question*: 'Lord, wilt thou at this time restore again the kingdom to Israel?' (1.6). Significantly, the Lord did not seek to correct their expectation of a restored Israel at the centre of the kingdom of God - He simply affirmed the sovereignty of the Father as to the timing of its inauguration. Jerusalem will yet be the centre around which affairs on earth will revolve during Christ's millennial kingdom, as anticipated by prophets such as Isaiah (Isa 2.1-5). With familiar grace, the Lord's response moved them on from something not for them to know to an *instruction* for their obedience: 'but... ye shall be witnesses unto me' (1.8). His final words before leaving earth clearly signalled the priority of witnessing. The Holy Spirit supplies the essential power for witness: 'ye shall receive power, after that the Holy Spirit is come upon you' (1.8). This was fulfilled on the Day of Pentecost (ch. 2) when the Holy Spirit descended to indwell believers and form the body of Christ. By contrast, the Spirit today indwells believers and adds them to the body of Christ at the moment of faith (Eph 1.13; 1 Cor 12.13). The Lord's plan for witnessing provides a table of contents for the book of Acts (1.8). The witness began in Jerusalem (ch. 1-7), spread to Judea and Samaria (ch. 8-12), and then to the uttermost part of the earth (ch. 13-28). A biblical approach to witnessing is therefore to start where we are and radiate outwards. Paul said to the Thessalonians: 'from you sounded out the word of the Lord' (1 Thess 1.8). Pause now to mark the change the Lord brought about in the twelve: the reality of the resurrection was no longer a question to them.

Ascension (vv9-12)

The climax of the 40-day period was the Lord's ascension into heaven. This provided **conclusive vindication** of His words, for John records at least seven occasions when the Lord alluded to leaving the world to return to the Father (Jn 14.12, 28; 16.5, 10, 16, 28; 17.11). At the tomb, the angel's message was, 'He is not here, but is risen: remember how He spake unto you when He was yet in Galilee?' (Lk 24.6). When Christ says something will happen, we may depend on it!

The ascension was also a **gracious provision** for the disciples. For the short period of time He dwelt among them, they had the unique experience of hearing, seeing, and handling the Son of God (1 Jn 1.1). But He did not leave them abruptly or without explanation. Instead, His slow-motion ascent into heaven, in their full view, gently moved them on from walking by sight to walking by faith (2 Cor 5.7).

The ascension was a step in Christ's **glorious exaltation**. He was 'taken up' (1.2, 11, 22; 1 Tim 3.16), indicating it was an honour done to Him by another. The direction He moved signalled His destination, as the repetition of the word 'heaven' four times in vv10, 11 emphasises. Long before the events of chapter 1, Isaiah had written of the suffering servant of Jehovah using three terms expressing promotion: 'He shall be exalted and be lifted up, and be very high' (Isa 52.13, JND). Christ's resurrection, ascension, and seating in glory answer well to Isaiah's prophecy, with each step constituting a further expression of the Father's delight in the work of His Son (2.33; Phi 2.8,9).

The ascension informs our **blessed expectation**. The angelic affirmation was, 'this same Jesus...shall so come in like manner as ye have seen Him go' (1.11). Christ's second coming to earth will be equally personal; He will not send a deputy, but descend Himself, first to the air for the church (1 Thess 4.16), then, after the events of the tribulation, to the earth. It will be physical, for He left in a human body from the mount of Olives (1.12), and at His return, 'His feet shall stand in that day upon the mount of Olives' – with earth-splitting consequences (Zech 14.4)! His return will be visible, not merely to a small gathering as at His ascension, but to 'all tribes of the earth' (Mt 24.30) and 'every eye' (Rev 1.7). May we live soberly, righteously, godly, in this present world, looking for that blessed hope, and the glorious appearing of the great God and our Saviour Jesus Christ (Titus 2.12,13)!

Supplication (vv13, 14)

The apostles spent the waiting time in Jerusalem in prayer, illustrating how best to 'wait on the Lord' (Isa 40.31). Their prayer meeting had **full participation**, for 'they all continued in prayer' (1.14). Significantly, Mary the mother of Jesus was there (1.14). Despite her privileged role in the nativity, her way of access to God was the same as every other believer. The Lord's brethren were there (1.14), indicating that they had been converted between the Feast of Tabernacles (Jn 7.5) and the resurrection. In addition to the apostles, the women were present (1.14). Audible prayer in the gatherings of the church is specifically committed to the males (1 Tim 2.8) hence what is expressed aloud is only a sample of the whole spiritual exercise. God alone hears the prayers of sisters, giving them an intrinsically precious quality. In contrast to the world's confusion of gender distinctions (Gen 1.27; Mt 19.4), it is fitting that in God's house, 'the pillar and ground of the truth' (1 Tim 3.15), His people worshipfully acknowledge His sovereign creatorial glory in the design and distribution of the two genders.

Their prayer meeting involved **united participation**, for they prayed 'with one accord' (1.14). The mob who came together to stone Stephen were united in wickedness (7.57), but godly harmony is good and pleasant (Ps 133.1), and worth cultivating (Rom 15.5-6).

Their prayer meeting had **purposeful participation**, for they made 'supplication' (1.14). Before praying, it is good to consider Ahasuerus' question to Esther, 'what is thy request' (Esther 5.3). James warns of three mistakes to avoid in prayer: swithering as to God's goodness – 'ask in faith, nothing wavering' (Jas 1.5-8); silence - 'ye have not because ye ask not' (Jas 4.2); and selfishness – 'ye ask, and receive not, because ye ask amiss, that ye may consume it upon your lusts' (Jas 4.3). Prayer meetings should be characterised by full, united, and purposeful participation, and by prayers that are expressed with confidence in God's goodness, and submission to His will.

Selection (vv15-26)

Judas was one of Christ's twelve disciples, a missionary to Israel, a miracle worker, the treasurer of the twelve – yet he was not a genuine believer. Little wonder Paul urged the Corinthians to 'Examine yourselves, whether ye be in the faith' (2 Cor 13.5). It is not wearisome for those who are saved by grace through faith to review the foundation of their salvation; it is safe (1 Jn 5.13, Phil 3.1,8-9). God used Peter, a restored backslider, to oversee the choice of Judas' replacement. Recovery to useful service is possible for the believer who stumbles, but those, like Judas, who decisively reject the Lord can only be removed.

The selection was approached **prayerfully**, In this spiritual atmosphere, Peter received clarity on how to deal with the situation created by Judas' betrayal (v12-14). As the proverb advises, 'commit thy works unto the LORD, and thy thoughts shall be established'

(Pr 16.3). The Lord prayed before He chose the twelve (Lk 6.12), and the apostles prayed before they chose a replacement for Judas (v24). Let us pray, then, before making significant decisions.

The selection was approached **scripturally**. Peter realised Psalm 69.25, which looks beyond its author David, anticipating the demise of all who set themselves against the Messiah, applied to the situation. He also quoted from Psalm 109.8, which references the swift removal and replacement of Messiah's treacherous enemy. Peter's total confidence in the *infallibility* of the word of God is demonstrated by his statement, 'this scripture must needs have been fulfilled' (1.16). What the scriptures say will happen must happen. The reason is their *inspiration*: 'the Holy Spirit by the mouth of David spake' (1.16). God has made Himself known by putting His words in men's mouths (or pens), under the direction of His Spirit. The Holy Spirit selected the very words, not simply the ideas. Accordingly, Paul could establish a doctrine on the distinction between a singular and a plural noun (Gal 3.16), and the Lord stated that the smallest letter of the law, or even part of a letter, would not go unfulfilled (Mt 5.18). Let us therefore have confidence in 'every word that proceedeth out of the mouth of God' (Mt 4.4).

Finally, the selection was approached **submissively**. Joseph and Matthias were identified as the two most qualified candidates, each having the correct length of acquaintance with Christ, and each having witnessed His resurrection (vv21,22; Jn 15.27). When the apostles had no further revelation to inform a decision between the two, they used the method of casting lots to select Matthias. This method was undertaken prayerfully, conscious of the sovereignty of God over even the smallest event on earth (Pr 16.33). A guiding principle emerges. We should proceed as far as possible based on what God has revealed in His word but, reaching a choice between equally valid options, we should make a reverent decision, confident in the Lord's sovereign overruling.

2

PENTECOST – THE DESCENT OF THE SPIRIT AND THE BIRTH OF THE CHURCH (2.1-47)

'Pentecost', also known as 'the Feast of Weeks' or 'the Feast of Harvest', was one of three annual celebrations Jewish men kept at Jerusalem (Ex 23.14-17; Dt 16.16). Occurring exactly fifty days (from which its name is derived) after Israel waved her first sheaf of the year before the Lord, it acknowledged God's harvest-time goodness (Ex 23.16; Lev 23.15-21; Num 28.26-31; Dt 16.9-12). Whether Israel realised it or not, it also looked forward to the coming of the Holy Spirit.

The time of its final fulfilment had arrived. That year, on the Day of Pentecost, when all the believers were gathered, fully united, in one place, 'suddenly there came a sound from heaven as of a rushing mighty wind, and it filled all the house where they were sitting. And there appeared unto them cloven tongues like as of fire, and it sat upon each of them' (2.1-3). Their unity pointed to the harmony which should have, though sadly has not, characterised Christ's churches (Jn 17.20, 21; 1 Cor 12.13; Gal 3.28). The suddenness of the Spirit's arrival showed just how quickly, when the time is right, God can accomplish His purposes. Speaking to Nicodemus, the Lord Jesus had likened the Spirit to the wind (Jn 3.8). And that is how He came, as 'a rushing mighty wind' (v2). The majestic sight of divided, fiery tongues sitting on each of the disciples further emphasised His unquenchable power (v3).

The Greek word *baptizō*, translated 'baptize', means to submerge.[1] John the Baptist predicted that Christ would baptize Israel 'with the Holy Ghost, and *with* fire' (Mt 3.11). Following His resurrection, the Saviour told His disciples, 'ye shall be baptized with the Holy Ghost not many days hence' (1.5). When, at Pentecost, the Spirit 'filled all the house where they were sitting', He immersed that small nucleus of 120 disciples, the first members of the Christian church and representatives of the entire body of Christ. That moment the church was born and, once and for all, baptized in the Spirit. Ever since, every repentant sinner, as soon as he or she has trusted Christ, has come into the good of what took place there, as though he or she was present on the Day of Pentecost (1 Cor 12.13). Spirit-baptism is not, therefore, a modern, post-conversion empowering of individual saints, but a historical, corporate experience of the entire church.

As well as baptising the disciples, the Holy Spirit filled them, supernaturally equipping them to speak, in recognizable human languages they had never learned, 'the wonderful works of God' (vv4, 11). News of the phenomenon spread quickly throughout Jerusalem, which at that time was full of devout Jews who had come from 'every nation under heaven' to keep the Feast of Pentecost (vv5, 6). When these heard the Galilean disciples speaking their own languages, they were simultaneously perplexed and amazed (vv6-11). Some asked genuinely what it meant; others scornfully accused them of drunkenness (vv12, 13).

Energized by the Holy Spirit, and standing with the other eleven apostles, Peter 'lifted up his voice', and, without reserve, spoke to the vast crowd. He addressed them nationally as 'men of Judaea ... all ye that dwell at Jerusalem ... ye men of Israel ... men and brethren ... all the house of Israel ...' (vv14, 22, 29, 36). He refuted the allegation that the disciples were drunk, explaining that this supernatural occurrence answered the prediction of the prophet Joel (vv15-21; Joel 2.18-22). Against the dark backdrop of the fearsome day of the Lord, Joel promised Israel that if she repented God would do great things for her (Joel 2.1, 12, 21). This included an outpouring of His Spirit on all flesh, so that her sons and daughters would prophesy, her old men dream dreams, and her young men see visions (Joel 2.28). What had just taken place in Jerusalem was a small foretaste of that still future outpouring, which will be accompanied by upheavals both terrestrial and celestial (Joel 2.30, 31).

Now fearless, Peter charged his Jewish audience with deliberately rejecting Jesus of Nazareth, a man of Whom God had shown His approval by divinely wrought 'miracles [*dunamis*, referring to their power] and wonders [*teras*, intimating the amazement they generated] and signs [*semeion*, telling of their spiritual significance]' (v22). It was true that Jesus had been delivered over to the suffering of the cross 'by the determinate counsel and foreknowledge of God', but, equally, Israel was guilty of crucifying and slaying Him (vv23, 36). Afterwards, because death could not hold Him, God raised Him from the dead (v24). Peter backed up this triumphant assertion with a quotation from Psalm 16. In that Psalm, David expressed complete trust in, devotion to, and delight in Jehovah. He went so far as to write that death itself could not disrupt his sweet fellowship with the Lord (vv25-28). But 1,000 years later, David was dead, though his tomb remained (v29). So, what did David's words refer to? Being a prophet, and confident that God would, according to His covenant, raise up of David's descendants the Messiah to sit on his throne, under the Holy Spirit's direction, David predicted Christ's resurrection. He even foresaw that while in the tomb the body of this Holy One would neither decay nor decompose (vv30, 31; cf. 2 Sam 7.1-17).

Peter and his fellow apostles were eyewitnesses of the fact that God had raised Jesus from the dead. They had also seen Him ascend into heaven (1.9, 11). Having been exalted by the right hand of

God, and received the Holy Spirit from the Father, He had poured out that same Spirit on His disciples (cf. Jn 7.39). Their unlearned ability to speak foreign languages was proof of this (v33). In Psalm 110, David spoke of a victorious Warrior-Priest-King Who, having been promoted to God's right hand, waited until His enemies were made His footstool (vv34, 35; Ps 110.1). Since David had not ascended into the heavens, these words also referred to Christ. When God raised Jesus of Nazareth from the dead and exalted Him to His own right hand, He reversed Israel's verdict on Him, declaring Him to be both Lord and Christ (v36).

In the Upper Room, the Lord Jesus had told His disciples that when the Spirit came, He would 'reprove the world of sin' (Jn 16.8). That is what He did now. Presented with these unassailable facts, the multitude 'were cut [*katanusso*, as 'the puncture of a spear'[2]] to the heart, and said to Peter and the rest of the apostles, "Brothers, what shall we do?"' (v37, ESV). Realization suddenly dawned – they were guilty of murdering Jesus the Messiah. Peter urged them to repent of this vile crime and, indeed, of all their misdemeanors, and, as a visible, outward symbol of the remission of their sins, be baptized in the name of Jesus Christ. If they did this, they too, like the 120 disciples, would receive the Holy Spirit (v38). This promise of forgiveness was offered to everyone; to those present, to their children and subsequent generations, to every Jew scattered throughout the world, to Gentiles, and to all whom God would call (v39). Peter said many other things, but, in summary, he counselled his hearers to save themselves 'from this crooked [*skolios*, from which we get the medical term scoliosis] generation' (v40, ESV).

Having heard Peter's word, 3,000 gladly received it, were baptized, and added to the church (v41). What they did afterwards formed a blueprint for church practice throughout this age. 'They continued stedfastly in the apostles' doctrine and fellowship, and in breaking of bread, and in prayers' (v42). These four activities are like the four legs of a table or chair. Remove one, and the whole structure collapses. Any local church which swerves from New Testament apostolic teaching, ceases to enjoy the sweetness of Christian fellowship, neglects the regular observance of the Lord's Supper, or stops having prayer meetings will invariably falter.

This sudden transformation of 3,000 people and their daily meeting together filled many with trepidation. Furthermore, through the 'many signs and wonders … done by the apostles', God actively validated their message (v43). With fresh enthusiasm for their newly found solidarity, the believers shared their possessions and resources, met daily in Herod's temple, ate meals and praised God together (vv44-47). For a very brief time, before persecution broke out, the new disciples were accepted by the people of Jerusalem. And with almighty power, 'the Lord added to the church daily such as should be saved' (v47). This He still does today.

3

ANOTHER OFFER OF THE KINGDOM, WHICH ISRAEL AGAIN REJECTED (3.1-4.37)

PETER AND JOHN were lifelong friends. Having fished on the Sea of Galilee together, and followed Christ together, now, at the 3 pm hour of prayer, they went to the temple together (3.1; cf. Lk 5.10). Intending to enter the Court of the Women after crossing the Court of the Gentiles, they approached the Beautiful Gate. Here they saw a familiar sight. A man in his forties, lame from birth, was asking alms of the temple worshippers. This he had done for many years (3.2; 4.22). Spotting Peter and John, he 'asked an alms' (3.3). That was all he expected, but when Peter, with rare intensity, fastened his eyes on him, saying, 'Look on us … he gave heed unto them' (3.4, 5). Having left his fishing business over three years earlier, Peter had no money. What he did have, however, was power. Therefore, having said to the man, 'In the name of Jesus Christ of Nazareth rise up and walk', he grasped him firmly 'by the right hand, and lifted him up: and immediately his feet and ankle bones received strength' (3.6, 7).

Disabled from birth, this man may have had a neurological or musculoskeletal condition. As well as experiencing muscle wasting and contractures, his prolonged immobility would have caused osteoporosis. Instantaneously, any deficiency of his neural functioning was corrected; weak and shortened muscles were fully strengthened, joint deformities righted, and his bone mineral density normalised. Feeling a sudden energy surge course through his body, the man jumped up and, walking, leaping, and praising God, entered the temple with Peter and John (3.8). This was

HEROD'S TEMPLE

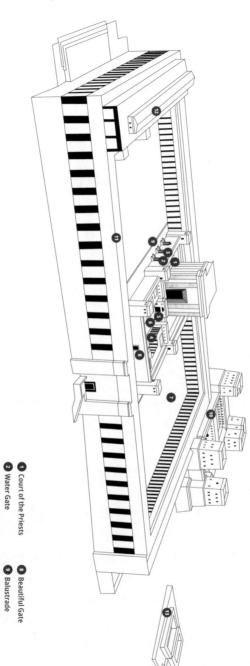

1. Court of the Priests
2. Water Gate
3. Gate of Firstlings
4. Court of the Women
5. Nicanor Gate
6. Chamber of Nazarites
7. Court of Gentiles
8. Beautiful Gate
9. Balustrade
10. Fort Antonia
11. Solomon's Porch
12. Royal Portico
13. Pool of Bethesda

exactly what Isaiah had predicted concerning the coming messianic kingdom – 'then shall the lame *man* leap as an hart' (Is 35.6). It was an amazing miracle which could not be refuted. Everyone who saw him walking and praising God knew he was the lame beggar, 'and they were filled with wonder and amazement at that which had happened unto him' (3.9, 10, 16). Even the Jewish leadership admitted the miracle was genuine (4.16).

When the people heard that the man was healed, they were astonished, and, wanting to see him for themselves, ran to Solomon's porch (3.11). Once more Peter preached to his nation. He began by claiming this miracle proved Jesus had risen from the dead (3.12-16). Next, on the strength of Old Testament prophecy, he called on his Jewish brothers to repent (3.17-24), concluding with a reminder of their great privileges (3.25, 26).

It was not Peter or John's personal power or holiness 'which made this man to walk' (3.12). Rather, it was their faith, and his faith, in the all-prevailing name of Jesus (3.16). Full of envy and spite, Israel's leaders had delivered Jesus to Pontius Pilate (3.13; cf. Mt 27.18; Mk 15.10). And when Pilate, having found no fault in Him, determined to release Him, they denied this Holy and Just One, desiring instead a murderer (3.13, 14; cf. Jn 19.4). In so doing, they became guilty of a transgression of monumental proportions, the killing of 'the Prince of life' (3.15). But the God of their forefathers, Abraham, Isaac, and Jacob, had raised His Servant Jesus from the dead and glorified Him (3.13, 15). Of this, Peter and John, with the other apostles, were eyewitnesses (3.15).

The book of Leviticus outlined the laws governing Old Testament sacrifices. It stipulated that if the whole nation sinned in ignorance, a sacrifice must be offered for their forgiveness (Lev 4.13-21). When Peter told his audience he was convinced they had crucified Christ in ignorance, he was holding out to them the real possibility of forgiveness (3.17). The Saviour took that same tack when He prayed, 'Father, forgive them; for they know not what they do' (Lk 23.34). Furthermore, their contribution to Christ's sufferings had, as predicted by the Old Testament prophets, unwittingly accomplished God's purpose (3.18). Peter therefore appealed to them to repent of their sins and turn to God (3.19). If they did this, there would be four amazing results –

- their sins would be blotted out (3.19; cf. Is 43.25) – this Greek word *exaleiphō* referred to 'the erasure of hand-writing'[3]
- a time of refreshing would come from the presence of the Lord (3.19; cf. Ps 72.6) – the Greek word *anapsuxis* meant a 'cooling, or reviving with fresh air'[4]
- Jesus Christ would return (3.20)
- there would be a restitution of all things (3.21) – the Greek word *apokatastasis*, used only here in the New Testament, was 'a technical medical term … [denoting] complete restoration of health'.[5]

This lame man's healing pictured God's final restoration of Israel and the whole universe at Messiah's Second Advent. In those days, the curse lifted and its effects reversed, the earth will be abundantly fruitful (Ps 72.16; Is 35.1, 7).

It was a remarkable offer! If Israel repented and believed the gospel, Christ would, as foretold by Moses, Samuel, and all the Old Testament prophets, return to inaugurate His world-wide kingdom, (3.21, 22, 24). If, however, they continued to reject Him (the Moses-like prophet), they would be destroyed (3.23). Alas, while many Jews accepted Jesus as Messiah, the nation as a whole refused Him (and still does), a decision leading to inevitable judgment. But their unbelief has not annulled God's promises for them; it has only delayed their accomplishment (Rom 11.25-36).

Peter concluded his sermon by reminding his audience they were the direct beneficiaries of the promises of the Old Testament prophets and the covenant God made with their father Abraham (3.25). They were Israelites, 'to whom *pertaineth* the adoption, and the glory, and the covenants, and the giving of the law, and the service *of God*, and the promises; whose *are* the fathers, and of whom as concerning the flesh Christ *came* ...' (Rom 9.4, 5). Through their nation Abraham's Descendant (Christ, in Whom every nation under heaven would be blessed) had come (3.25). Appropriately, they were the first to hear the gospel. Having raised His Servant from the dead, God sent the apostles to preach Jesus to the Jews, that they might turn from their iniquities (3.26).

Peter's message received an immediate response. Positively, about 5,000 believed (4.4). Negatively, grieved that Peter and John 'preached through Jesus the resurrection from the dead', the priests, the captain of the temple (responsible for its security), and the Sadducees (who rejected the idea of resurrection) imprisoned both the two apostles and the man who had been healed (4.1, 2, 14). The next day, they set them before the Sanhedrin, the supreme Jewish court of justice, the same council which had plotted against, tried, and wrongfully convicted Christ (Mt 26.3, 66). As far as the Sanhedrin was concerned, Peter and John, lacking formal religious training and recognition, were 'unlearned and ignorant men' (4.13). But when Peter, undaunted by their august assemblage, spoke with Spirit-borne boldness, they were stunned, recognising that 'they had been with Jesus' (4.13). Peter emphasized that the healing of the lame man was a 'good deed', deserving neither arrest nor punishment (4.9). Broadening his answer beyond the Sanhedrin 'to all the people of Israel', he accused the entire nation of crucifying 'Jesus Christ of Nazareth, ... whom God raised from the dead' (4.10). It was only through Jesus' name and power that the lame man had been made whole (4.10). In other words, his healing was proof that Jesus Christ had risen from the dead.

Israel's religious leaders were duty-bound to build up the nation. Instead, they had rejected God's Messiah as a defective stone. By exalting Jesus of Nazareth to the highest possible place, God overturned their ruling (4.11; cf. Ps 118.22; Mt 21.33-46; Eph 2.20-22). Now in heaven, Jesus Christ is the only Saviour through Whom 'we must be saved' (4.12).

Unable to deny the veracity of the miracle, or hide it, the Sanhedrin simply warned Peter and John to stop speaking and teaching in Jesus' name (4.14-18). But Peter, feeling an irresistible, divinely generated compulsion to tell all he had seen and heard, and sensing God's ever watchful gaze, refused to be silent (4.19, 20). Fearing public opinion, the council reiterated their threat, then released the two apostles (4.21-23).

Freed, Peter and John made a beeline for the believers, to whom they 'reported all that the chief priests and elders had said unto them' (v23). The disciples were not angered by the Sanhedrin's threats, nor paralysed through fear. Instead, they prayed (4.24-31). Lifting 'up their voice to God with one accord', they worshipped Him as the all-powerful Creator, applied Holy Scripture (the second Psalm) to their own situation, and recognised that the malicious machinations of men had merely fulfilled God's plan (4.24-28). They did not plead for their enemies to be destroyed, nor for protection from them. Rather, they asked the Lord to notice how they, His servants, were being threatened, and, in light of this, to give them courage to speak His word (4.29). Selflessly, they prayed for God to stretch out His almighty hand to heal, so that signs and wonders would be done by His now resurrected Holy Servant Jesus (4.30). God began to answer their prayer by shaking the place, filling them with the Holy Spirit, and enabling them to speak His word boldly (4.31).

The oneness of the believers extended beyond this first recorded Christian prayer meeting to an altruistic, practical support of each other (4.32-37; cf. Jn 15.12). Barnabas, for example, was one of many who sold lands and houses to meet the physical needs of others (4.34-37; cf. 2 Cor 8.13, 14). This harmony contributed to the apostles' powerful witness to Christ's resurrection and collective enjoyment of God's grace (4.33). While it is unlikely God will now physically shake the buildings in which local churches gather, if we want to know His power we need to be united and generous in our interactions with each other.

4

PURGING THE CHURCH AND
PRESERVING THE SERVANTS (5.1-42)

'OUR GOD IS A CONSUMING FIRE' (Heb 12.29). At Sinai, He slew
Nadab and Abihu for offering strange fire before Him (Lev 10.1-
3). At Jericho, He summarily punished Achan for theft (Josh 7.21,
24, 25). Here, at the beginning of the church age, the Lord killed
Ananias and Sapphira for faking a Spirit-inspired generosity (4.34,
35; 5.1-11).

Prompted by Satan (rather than the Spirit), Ananias and Sapphira
plotted to sell a possession, withhold some of the money, but lay the
remainder at the apostles' feet as though they had given all (vv1, 2,
4, 9). In other words, they lied to look good. But their attempted
deception of the apostles was lying to, and tempting the Holy Spirit
of the Lord Who indwells every child of God (vv3, 4, 9; cf. Num
14.22; Ps 51.4). Divinely equipped, Peter exposed and punished
their wickedness so that, in an ironic twist, they died where they
had sinned – at the apostles' feet (vv3–6, 8-10). Unsurprisingly, this
caused 'great fear' within and without the church (vv5, 11).

In answer to the believers' prayer (as recorded in chapter 4),
'many signs and wonders' were done by the apostles (4.30; 5.12).
People weakened by illness were strengthened; others, distressed by
demons, were liberated. Desperate for healing, the sick of Jerusalem
were brought into her streets, and many from surrounding cities
were drawn into the capital (vv15, 16). This initial explosion of
the miraculous was another glorious foretaste of Christ's future
millennial rule (Heb 6.5b). It also filled people with fear. While
more and more were 'added to the Lord' and met with the other

converts in Solomon's Porch, unbelievers were wary of joining this new and powerful movement (vv12-14).

Filled with envy at this overwhelming demonstration of power, the high priest and his fellow Sadducees jailed the apostles (vv17,18). That night, however, an angel released them and commanded them to return to the temple and continue speaking their life-containing message about the living Christ (vv17-20). Early in the morning, as they obediently reentered the temple and taught the people, the Sanhedrin ordered the apostles be brought before them (v21). The discovery of an empty prison cell had filled the council with consternation (vv22-24). As they contemplated its implications, they were told that the very apostles they had imprisoned were now standing in the temple and freely 'teaching the people' (v25). Promptly, they sent their officials to arrest the apostles once more, but carefully, because of their popularity with the crowd (v26).

For the second time, the apostles stood before the Sanhedrin and an irate high priest (v27). Infuriated that his authority had been flouted yet unwilling to verbalize the name of 'Jesus', Annas challenged what he viewed as defiant public teaching 'in this name' (v28). In a remarkable testimony to the effectiveness of the apostles' witness, Annas accused them of filling Jerusalem with their doctrine (v28). We might ask ourselves if we have filled our neighbourhoods with the gospel of Jesus Christ. Finally, the high priest charged the apostles with blaming this most highly esteemed Jewish council for the death of Jesus of Nazareth. This was a classic example of twisting a narrative. After all, this very body of men had moved the people to cry out to Pilate concerning Christ, 'His blood be on us, and on our children' (Mt 27.25). The Sanhedrin seem to have been genuinely concerned lest the apostles' preaching whip up a frenzied attack on them.

The apostles' answer was a model defence of the gospel. They asserted that the divine command to preach trumped any human restriction (v29). While foregrounding the cross, resurrection, and exaltation of Jesus, they exposed the horrific sin of their audience (vv30, 31). This imposing council was accountable for slaying God's Messiah, hanging Him on a tree, and thus exposing Him to the divine curse (v30; Deut 21.22, 23; Gal 3.13). And yet Israel, guilty of such wrongdoing, was offered repentance and forgiveness (v31). The apostles, together with the Holy Spirit, bore witness to these irrefutable facts (v32).

Cut to the heart by the message, the council contemplated killing the messengers (v33). However, as this murderous thought sizzled through their ranks, Gamaliel, a highly respected Pharisee and teacher of the law, counselled a different approach (v34; cf. 22.3). There are two common responses to any threat: attack it with vigour or leave it alone. Gamaliel suggested the second. Citing two recent political examples, he counselled ignoring the apostles (vv34-37). If their preaching was not of God, it would soon fizzle out (v38). If, on the other hand, this new movement had divine endorsement, no power on earth could stop it (v39). The council agreed with Gamaliel and released their prisoners, having beaten and banned them from speaking any more in Jesus' name (v40). In this way, God used a leading Pharisee to save the lives of His servants. Far from being discouraged by a beating, they rejoiced at the privilege of suffering for Christ's sake and continued their evangelistic ministry (v42; 1 Pet 4.13, 14).

5
PRACTICALITIES AND PRIORITIES IN THE CHURCH (6.1-7)

Luke has consistently attributed the increase in number of disciples to the hand of the Lord (2.47, 5.14); this is the implication again as disciples continued to be 'multiplied' (v1). God works hand in hand with human agency. This miraculous work of salvation was possible because of the reprieve granted by Gamaliel (5.38) and the apostles' continued fervour in preaching the gospel (5.42). Sadly, blessing in salvation never comes without opposition. As Paul wrote to the Corinthians, 'a great door and effectual is opened … and there are many adversaries' (1 Cor 16.9). Through Ananias and Sapphira, Satan attempted to corrupt the church from within (5.3); the Jewish religious system (the world) opposed the spread of the gospel from without (5.18, 28). Now the flesh – the old sinful disposition in every believer – troubled the Jerusalem assembly. These common enemies are still opposed to the Lord and His people today.

The Problem
Just as the dispensation of Law commenced with discontent (Ex 16.2) which brought severe judgment upon Israel, 'murmuring' (v1) now threatened to derail the dispensation of grace. Sins of the flesh appear small but can rapidly become highly destructive; they need to be mortified, since 'little foxes … spoil the vines' (Song 2.15). 'A mixed multitude' had hampered Israel's wilderness progress (Ex 12.38); disaffection between Greek-speaking Jews of the *diaspora* and Hebrew-speaking Jews of Israel had the potential to subvert

the advance of the gospel. Even though the Hellenist and Hebrew Jews had been saved and become 'one new man' in Christ Jesus (Eph 2.15), ethnic rivalries remained.

Lamentably, the same hypocrisy can be true of us. What we are in Christ should be seen in daily life. Cultural, ethnic, and linguistic differences should not be allowed to cause disharmony between those who are one in Christ. Since He has once and for all 'made peace through the blood of his cross' (Col 1.20), we should make every effort to preserve such a costly unity.

The grumbling arose because the Hellenists felt that their widows had been neglected (v1). We are not told if this was real or perceived discrimination. The early disciples had all things common, and some had voluntarily sold their possessions for the benefit of others in need (2.44; 4.37). This was not a form of Christian socialism but rather the meeting of a particular practical need in the unique circumstances of the early church period. Believers are not mandated to have all things common today, since the Acts narrative is not necessarily prescriptive. However, we should still do good to the household of faith. The common fund of the early Jerusalem Christians, probably including food and other provisions, was distributed according to need. One group of beneficiaries were widows, but some, it seemed, were being overlooked in the daily distribution.

Although Scripture does not demand that we share a common fund with other Christians, we are specifically commanded to care for widows. Paul makes clear to Timothy that this responsibility falls first to the nearest saved family relatives, any failure to do so being tantamount to denying the faith (1 Tim 5.8). If there are no relatives available, then care for recognised widows falls to the local assembly (1Tim 5.9). Translating this into 21st century language means that elderly saints should in the normal course of things be cared for by their immediate family and not abandoned to care homes. Since God is 'a judge of the widows' (Ps 68.5) we should emulate His fatherly care. In some cases, this ideal cannot be met due to severe health problems, and practical wisdom dictates that specialist care is needed.

The Solution

'The twelve' moved quickly to solve the problem. As corrosive as grumbling and neglect can be, the invisible enemy is often a more dangerous foe. The subtle error which raised its head here was the temptation to let physical provision take precedence over spiritual activity and gospel work. 'To have allowed social relief to take over to the exclusion of evangelism would have been a criminal dereliction of duty to both God and man …… It can so easily happen that social activities become the cuckoo in the nest and virtually oust the preaching of the word and prayer.'[6] There is biblical precedent for charitable work, but to place social enterprise on an equal footing with preaching and prayer is spiritually fatal. Certainly, the early believers were active in good works. The apostle Peter healed many sick (5.15). Dorcas was known for her charity (9.36). When Paul left Jerusalem, he was commanded to 'remember the poor' (Gal 2.10). Such deeds of mercy played a supporting role in the advance of the gospel, but they did not replace it. Western culture overflows with seemingly legitimate 'social issues', but we dare not start down endless rabbit holes that divert attention away from the great commission. Our mandate is not to make people on the broad road more affluent but to warn them to flee from the wrath to come. The words of the apostles still ring true – 'it is not reason that we should leave the word of God, and serve tables' (v2).

The apostles were not passive bystanders but sturdy leaders who 'called the multitude of the disciples unto them' and spelled out the problem (v2). Realising the limitations of their own energy and time, they had to prioritise their own duty in teaching the word of God. Moses could not act as sole administrator for the entire congregation of Israel (Ex 18.13) and simultaneously mediate for the people 'God-ward' (Ex 18.19). He had to appoint others to address social disputes (Ex 18.22). Similarly, while the apostles engaged in spiritual activity, they delegated others to meet the physical needs of the saints. Each Christian has a unique sphere of service in which he or she is expected to labour. The Lord Jesus told Peter to concentrate on his own service, not to mind John's (Jn 21.22). The same applies to us.

Assembly servants should be of exemplary character (1 Tim 3.8-13). The instruction to 'look … out among you seven men' (v3) was not an exercise in democracy. The assembly was simply recognising spiritual men who could be trusted to steward monetary affairs. In a similar vein, Paul wrote about 'the brother whose praise is in the gospel throughout all the churches … who was also chosen of the churches to travel with us with this [gift]' (2 Cor 8.19). God gifts individuals and raises up overseers, but an assembly must recognise capable men who can administer its material affairs (1 Cor 16.3).

These servants had to be men (*aner*, a male). Christian women serve God invaluably, but Scripture teaches consistently that in a local church leadership responsibility lies with the men. This reflects God's creatorial design. Man was created to lead, bear responsibility and be the head of the woman (1 Cor 11.3).

When God appoints men to serve His people, He is interested neither in their academic achievements nor their managerial credentials. The men in Acts 6 had to be 'accredited' (v3, Wuest) in the sense of having a proven track-record in faithfulness. The list of qualifications for a servant are outlined in 1 Timothy; a servant of the church must be 'proved' before he can serve (1 Tim 3.10).

Such men were to be full of the Holy Spirit and wisdom (v3). This was exemplified in the case of Joseph, who was in touch with God, interpreted dreams, but also suggested a practical solution to the imminent seven-year famine facing Egypt (Gen 41). Similarly, the seven men of Acts 6 were qualified spiritually and practically.

Having dealt with a carnal problem by spiritual means, the apostles devoted themselves to prayer and the word (v4). They knew that they did not 'war after the flesh' (2 Cor 10.3). They wrestled 'against principalities, against powers, against the rulers of the darkness of this world, against spiritual wickedness in high *places*' (Eph 6.12). The gospel would progress as they spent time on their knees. 'Ministry [*diakonia*] of the word' (v4) is the noun for the verbal form of 'serve [*diakoneo*] tables' (v2). Whilst there is a clear emphasis in the passage on spiritual and evangelistic activity taking precedence over charitable works, the 'sacred / secular' divide must not be overly pressed. Every aspect of the Christian life is a spiritual service of sorts, comprehending the mundane and the sacred. They are not dichotomous categories in constant competition; both in their proper place work in harmony to please the Lord.

Stephen and Philip stand out amongst the seven (v5). Before attaining the limelight (Stephen in chapter 7 and Philip in chapter 8) they served behind the scenes. This principle of being faithful in little before being entrusted with much is highly pertinent (Lk 16.10-12). The choice of the assembly was ratified by the apostles when 'they laid their hands on them' (v6). This simple act showed that the seven had the blessing of the apostles, who unbegrudgingly committed them to this work.

It was then that 'the word of God kept on increasing and … the disciples … kept on multiplying' (v7[7]). Luke repeatedly makes the point that God blesses those who are fit for blessing, corporately and individually (2.47; 4.32-35; 5.11-14). When, therefore, the apostles gave themselves to prayer and the word, blessing in salvation followed. Let us pray that the Lord will help us recapture these basic principles and, in the power of the Spirit, live them out.

'Obedient to the faith' (v7) 'denotes the testimony of the gospel, which is most worthy of belief … in other passages the expression is used, "to obey the gospel" (Rom 10.16; 2 Thess 1.8), and thence, obedience to the faith (Rom 1.5; Rom 16.26)'.[8] The gospel message is an authoritative, non-negotiable, command from God to obey His word. May we preach it to all and sundry.

6

STEPHEN, THE FIRST CHRISTIAN MARTYR (6.8-7.60)

THE FABRICATION THAT BROUGHT STEPHEN before the Sanhedrin was that he blasphemed Moses and God (6.11). These allegations were then formalised by false witnesses; the official charges being, that Stephen blasphemed the temple and the law.

Despite false accusations, Stephen didn't speak against the law or the temple – he had the highest regard for both. However, he knew they were not God's final revelation, and neither could save from sin. The law was a schoolmaster until Christ came (Gal 3.24) and since the Messiah had died and risen, God was showing the nation that it was time to move on. Alas, they stubbornly refused.

A point of debate here is the nature of God's revelation. He reveals himself progressively. He does not speak all at once, but like the placement of stepping stones, he speaks one step at a time, and expects his people to follow. Stone two is not the same as stone one, but a man cannot reach stone two without first stepping on stone two. Although the stones are different, they do not contradict each other. There is progression, fulfilment, and complementarity between the stones. When stood on stone two a man must look to move to stone three; there is no need to cling on to or return to stone one, since it has served its purpose. The nature of God's revelation is woven into Stephen's defence. The law was a stepping stone to the Messiah. He had come and the Jewish nation needed to move on to Him, which would entail leaving the law behind. Stephen's address shows the folly of ignoring God's progressive revelation.

Stephen was asked straightly, 'are these things so?' (7.1). His answer was an historical overview, using key aspects of Israel's history as doctrinal goads to prod his audience (9.5). By considering the nation's past, Stephen did the following:

1) Refuted the charges of blaspheming the temple and the law
   Disproved the accusation of speaking against God and Moses
2) Showed that God's revelation is progressive
3) Demonstrated that God keeps His word
4) Proved that God's presence is not restricted to a single location
5) Exposed Israel's habitual refusal to accept God's deliverer

Most of Stephen's address can be interpreted in light of these criteria.

Abraham (vv1-8)

Far from blaspheming God, Stephen called Him 'the God of the glory' (7.1, YLT). His theology proper, is completely orthodox, as he calls God, the Lord (7.31, 33, 37), the angel of the Lord (7.30), the God of the Patriarchs (7.32), the Most High (7.48), and the Holy Ghost (7.51) throughout his address.

By saying that God appeared in pagan Mesopotamia Stephen is hammering from the off the Jewish obsession that God's presence was confined to Jerusalem. The Jews thought that they had a monopoly on God, and since his name was set in Jerusalem (2 Chr 6.6; Ps 132.13), that guaranteed salvation for them. They could not have been more wrong. Stephen had never spoken against the holy place, in the sense of calling for the destruction of the physical temple. But in preaching the gospel, he had fundamentally undermined its spiritual foundation. The death and resurrection of the Lord Jesus had rendered the temple system obsolete. The vail had been rent (Mk 15.38), a new temple had been raised (Jn 2.19), the rejected stone was now the head of the corner (Lk 20.17). It was, therefore, time to worship God in Spirit, not in Jerusalem (Jn 4.24). In calling the Jews to leave the law and embrace Christ, Stephen was calling them to leave the locus of their religious centre. He was saying that the temple was a fine monument of the past, but God's presence had moved out. They could now leave the shadows, because the substance - One greater than the temple – had come (Mt 12.6). Stephen proved from Jewish history that God's presence had regularly moved and had never been confined to the bricks of Jerusalem. God had appeared in heathen Ur of the Chaldees, in Egypt (7.9), in a desert thorn bush (7.30), and Gentile Canaan (7.45). If God had located His presence outside Jerusalem before, He could do so again. It was time for the Jews to abandon the temple system, and join the church, the temple of the living God (1 Cor 3.17).

Stephen added new information to previous revelation; although Abraham was called in Ur of the Chaldees, initially he only made it to Haran. His father Terah was a hindrance, for it was only after his death that Abraham entered Canaan. Stephen said this because a new revelation from God is often followed by faltering obedience. God helped Abraham on the way when He 'removed him' (7.4) from Haran. God wanted to help the Jews by removing them from Judaism, but they stubbornly clung to shadows.

God gave Abrahm a promise (7.5), a prophetic timetable (7.6), and proof when His word would be fulfilled: 'they shall serve me in this place' (7.7). Israel could trace the validity of God's revelation through the centuries and see if He was good on His word. God had given the current generation of Jews, a promise, a prophetic timetable, and climactic proof in the resurrection of His Son. It is impossible for God to lie, and He had kept His word supremely in the death and resurrection of the Lord Jesus. The Jews had no excuse for disobedience because God's word had been proven absolutely true.

Stephen emphasised how Abraham simply relied on a spoken promise when he had no land to call his own, and no child (7.5). In contrast, the Jews had ample tangible evidence (signs, cf. Jn 20.30-31) upon which to trust. Faith is the only fitting response to God's revelation. Without faith it is impossible to please him (Heb 11.6).

God also revealed that Israel would become slaves in Egypt (7.6). This becomes significant when Jacob is called by Joseph to enter Egypt (7.14-15) and later when Moses predicts the coming of Messiah (7.37). God gives advance notice of a change in revelation. Originally God had prohibited Isaac from going to Egypt (Gen 26.2), a command that Jacob followed. When the famine struck, Jacob didn't go to Egypt himself (in obedience to prior revelation) but sent his sons 'first' (7.12). However, he was then summoned by Joseph (7.14-15). Would he stay or go? Would going entail disobedience to prior revelation? A few things helped dislodge Jacob from the comfort of his tent:

- A saviour had gone before: 'God did send me before you to preserve life (Gen 45.5)
- He was summoned by the saviour: 'Thus saith ... Joseph, God hath made me lord of all Egypt: come down unto me' (Gen 45.9)
- He was warned about disobedience: 'There are five years of famine; lest thou ... come to poverty' (Gen 45.11)
- There was blessing and glory if he obeyed: 'Ye shall tell my father of all my glory in Egypt' (Gen 45.13)
- Evidence was provided to aid his obedience: 'To his father he sent ... asses laden with the good things of Egypt' (Gen 45.23)
- New revelation was given to supersede the previous prohibition: 'Fear not to go down into Egypt ... I will go down with thee ... and I will ... bring thee up again' (Gen 46.3-4)
- The new command had been given advanced notice: Israel 'should sojourn in a strange land ... [be brought] into bondage

… after that shall they come forth, and serve me in this place' (Gen 15.13-16; Acts 7.6-7)

Despite Isaac being warned not to travel to Egypt, God now signalled to Jacob that it was time to move. It would have been folly for Jacob to disobey. This principle applied to the Jews of AD 33. The Sinaitic law was only a schoolmaster until Christ came. God had made clear in the resurrection of Christ, that the schoolmaster had served his purpose, and Israel was to leave it and follow the Lord Jesus.

Joseph (vv9-16)

Stephen now weaves the motif of rejection into his argument. Israel had repeatedly refused God's chosen deliverers. 'The patriarchs … sold Joseph into Egypt' (7.9) and later spurned Moses (7.25, 26, 35, 39). This climaxed in their rejection of Christ (7.52).

Stephen uses Joseph as a type of Christ; both were 'sold … delivered … and made … ruler(s)'. Having betrayed their sibling, Joseph's brothers' eyes were opened on their 'second' visit to Egypt (7.13). Fast-forward to AD 33 and the resurrection of Christ offered Israel a second opportunity. Tragically, instead of acknowledging their guilt, they hardened their hearts.

Moses – part 1 (vv17-28)

Stephen divides Moses' life into 40-year periods: Egypt (7.17-28), Midian (7.29-34), and the wilderness (7.35-44). Stephen refuted the charge that he blasphemed Moses by reciting an orthodox view of the prophet, showing he was divinely favoured (7.12), and presenting him as a Messianic prototype (7.35, 37). Far from blaspheming Moses, Stephen believed him (Jn 5.46). Moses wrote of Christ, and Stephen was following his writings, unlike the current Jews.

The prophetic clock for leaving Egypt was chiming (7.6, 17), and God made it obvious to the nation when they had to move. 'God had given clear instruction for Israel to go into Egypt, but this was a temporary arrangement. Stephen made it abundantly clear that the successive stages in God's … revelation were always consistent with … his original purpose, the advent of a new stage in that revelation required Israel to begin acting in a different way … A child who has been taught by means of coloured bricks the basic arithmetical principles of addition … will not be abandoning that basic principle when he moves on from bricks to computers. But he will abandon the bricks.'[9]

Stephen presents Moses as the deliverer (7.25), viewing Israel as his brethren (7.23), being grieved by their oppression (7.24), and expecting them to acknowledge him as their emancipator (7.25). This is almost Johannine: 'He came unto his own, and his own received him not' (Jn 1.11). Moses is normally criticised for this attempt to deliver Israel as a 40-year-old man, but Stephen places the blame at the feet of the nation. Their failure to understand (7.25) caused them to 'thrust [him] away' (7.27). Similarly, the Jews of AD 33 were wilfully ignorant of the Lord Jesus and rejected the Saviour (7.25, 27).

Moses – part 2 (vv29-35)

Stephen foregrounds the Gentile geography that dominated Moses' life. He lived in Midian (7.29), called his son Gershom (meaning 'a stranger in a strange land') (Ex 2.22), and used the word holy place (*topos*) (cf. 6.14; 7.7, 33, 49), to refer to ground in the Sinai desert. Clearly, God could meet with His people anywhere He chose. This was a vital truth to cherish as the gospel spread and assemblies formed across the Mediterranean world. God was pleased to meet with those who gathered to the name of the Lord Jesus (Mt 18.20) anywhere on planet earth.

Moses – part 3 (vv35-44)

Moses came to a people groaning under slavery (7.34). Stephen parallels Moses with the Lord Jesus, showing that although both were redeemers and miracle workers (2.22; 7.36), each was ultimately 'refused' (3.14; 7.35). Stephen quotes the Messianic prediction of a coming Moses-like prophet (7.37); 'the LORD ... will raise up ... a Prophet '(Deut 18.15). 'Stephen ... noted that Moses ... predicted that a Prophet like himself would appear ... the Jews [therefore] should not have concluded that the Mosaic Law was the end of God's revelation to them.'[10]

Israel's second and ultimate rejection of Moses (7.27, 39) came at the borders of the promised land, when they wanted to stone Moses (Num 14.10) and return to their old way of life in Egypt. The parallel with the Lord Jesus is clear. Although Christ was first refused by the nation at Calvary, He was now giving the nation another opportunity through Stephen. They were on the border of millennial blessing and had a choice to make. Would they accept the invitation, or go back to their old way of life in bondage to the law? Alas, as they stoned Stephen and apostatised, history repeated itself.

Accused of disregarding the law (6.13-14), Stephen reversed the charge against his accusers, showing that the children like their fathers in the wilderness were law breakers. When the law was inaugurated, Israel wanted Aaron to make them gods (7.38-40). Just as Israel's first high priest was embroiled in idolatry in the wilderness, history was repeating itself, in that the religious class was leading the people away from God. By rejecting God's mediator and rejoicing 'in the work of their own hands' (7.41), the Jews of the Exodus descended into idolatry. Similarly, the Jews of AD 33 had hand made their own idol, and wanted to follow it, instead of the Mediator (1 Tim 2.5). They had sculpted an idol out of the law, by keeping the external elements like the stones of the temple and the animal sacrifices. Their idol had a thin veneer of reality that may at quick glance have fooled some into thinking it was the real law. However, behind the wallpaper sat cavernous cracks of falsehood. This was not the divine law that pointed people to Christ, but an idolatrous sham that damned souls (Mt 23.15). They used their law keeping as a pretext for rejecting Christ. They paid lip service to God, but their hearts were far away from Him. Such idolatry must be abolished (1 Jn 5.21).

Stephen has regularly condensed parts of Israel's history into a few phrases (7.8, 16, 36, 39). This is repeated when he speaks of God giving them up to worship the host of heaven (7.42). This compact statement which seems to relate to the wilderness initially actually covers the whole life cycle of the nation from the wilderness through to Babylonian captivity. Israel had a penchant for worshiping the constellations, whether at its commencement (Deut 4.19) or immediately prior to its destruction: 'all the houses upon whose roofs they have burned incense unto all the host of heaven' (Jer 19.13). The 40 years that Stephen quotes from Amos is used representatively as the number of divine testing. The nation had been tested from the days of Moses through to the days of Jeremaih. They had failed the test, so God dispersed the nation.

Stephen presses home the extent of their idolatry by saying, 'ye took up the tabernacle of Moloch' (v43). Such was their idolatry, it was as if they carried a heathen god. The 'tabernacle of Moloch' indicates corporate idolatry, while the 'star of Remphan' could refer to a smaller symbol kept in the home. Privately and publicly, they were corrupt. This idolatry resulted in the Babylonian captivity (v43). Prophesying to the northern kingdom, Amos wrote, 'therefore will I cause you to go into captivity beyond Damascus, saith ... the God of hosts' (Amos 5.27). Stephen applies Amos' quotation to the Babylonian captivity, showing that the southern kingdom had been judged for idolatry before, and that the current crop of Judaean leaders were in danger of leading the Jewish people into a global dispersion again.

By appealing to the Babylonian captivity Stephen was tacitly reminding them that Solomon's temple had not survived God's judgement. If they continued to refuse Christ, then the temple would provide no shelter for them from the wrath of God. In fact, not a stone would be left on another (Lk 21.6).

The holy place (vv44-53)

Stephen countered the charge that he spoke against the temple, by saying that the tabernacle was made according to the 'fashion' (7.44). That is to say, he revered the divine design. However, Stephen knew that it was a design for a past dispensation, a point the Jews struggled to grasp.

As the ark entered 'the possession of the Gentiles', Stephen proves that God had not yet revealed Jerusalem as the place where he would dwell (Ps 132.13). The idea of progressive revelation applies to the dwelling place of God. Initially God moved around the wilderness and Canaan land in a tent. This is where He met with Israel. However, He gave them advanced notice that the tabernacle system would change when He placed His name in a more permanent place (Deut 12.5). God had changed His meeting place in the dispensation of law, and was doing it again in the dispensation of grace. He had dwelt in Gentile territory before and was about to do it again. All this shows the Jewish obsession with Jerusalem was idolatrous. God's presence had moved from Jerusalem (Jn 4.21), and He was now dwelling among local assemblies. The Jews needed to realise that because the Messiah had come and was building the church, they should leave the temple system and meet with Christ outside the camp (Heb 13.13).

Stephen's brief reference to the temple – 'Solomon built him an house' (7.47) - emphasised that God is greater than the building. Just as Israel made an idol out of the brazen serpent (2 Kings 18.4) they would idolise the temple, and thus Stephen contrasts the temporary, transient building with the eternal transcendent creator of the universe (7.48-50).

Conclusion (vv51-53)

After weaving the tapestry of Israel's history in a way that vindicated his position and condemned the Sanhedrin, Stephen spells out the sins of the nation. Shifting from the first-person plural 'we', to the second person plural 'ye', Stephen lays the blame squarely on the Sanhedrin as the nation's representatives.[11]

They were as stiff-necked as their fathers (Ex 33.3, 5; 34.9). The Sanhedrin boasted in circumcision, hoping that links to Abraham would save them, yet Stephen scathingly calls them 'uncircumcised in heart' (7.51). The physical sign did not reflect the spiritual reality (Deut 10.16).

Just as their fathers had resisted God in the wilderness (Num 27.14), they opposed God's Son and Spirit. Nationally, their rejection of the Triune God was total.

Stephen stands as the climactic prophet in Israel's history, joining Isaiah and Nehemiah in declaring that they were resisting the Holy Spirit; 'they rebelled, and vexed his holy Spirit' (Is 63.10); 'many years thou … testifiedst against them by thy Spirit … yet would they not give ear' (Neh 9.30).

Stephen, in using the title 'Just One', shows that only Christ kept the law, satisfied its claims at the cross, and was raised again for the justification of His people. The only hope the Jews had of righteousness, was by letting go of the law keeping that condemned them and embrace Christ – the Justifying One.

Just as their fathers had received revelation from God through angelic ministry (7.53) this generation saw Stephen's face as an angel (6.15). Angelic ministry is often associated with divine revelation (Gal 3.19) meaning, when the Jews saw Stephen's angelic face they knew that he was God's messenger and they would be held accountable for how they responded.

The stoning (vv54-60)

His scathing rebuke cut the heart of the Sanhedrin (7.54). Instead of repenting, they 'gnashed with their teeth'. Just like Gabbatha when the crowd cried out for the crucifixion of Stephen's Master (Mk 15.14; Jn 19.16), the same was happening again. They hated Christ and Stephen (Jn 15.18). Stephen imitated the conduct of his Lord. He viewed present suffering in the light of coming glory (Lk 24.26). Just as the Lord saw heaven opened prior to Calvary (Jn 12.28), Stephen follows in His path. The glory of God and Jesus are equated. A man seen seated where only God can be enthroned testifies to the deity of Christ. 'Son of man' is a divine title (Dan 7.13-14) which must have reminded the Jews of One who would reign in righteousness, because the Son of man would give 'judgement … to the saints of the Most High' (Dan 7.22). Stephen knew his cause would eventually be vindicated.

As the stones rained down on Stephen, 'he was praying … Lord Jesus, receive my spirit' (v59, JND). Resembling his Lord (Lk 23.46), he committed his life to One who judges righteously (1 Pet 2.23). Just as the Lord prayed that His crucifixion would not be chargeable to the Jews (Lk 23.34), Stephen prays in similar fashion. He fell asleep in Christ (7.60). Stephen died as a martyr full of faith. He feared neither stoning nor the wrath of man. He embraced death as a gateway to paradise. His spirit would soar into the heavenly temple, while his battered body awaited the day when 'the dead in Christ rise first'. He had finished his course and kept the faith (2 Tim 4.7). As the Lord stood to greet the first martyr, Stephen enjoyed a victor's entrance into glory. May we follow his courage and be faithful unto death (Rev 2.10).

Comparing Moses with Stephen

	Common Principle	Moses	Stephen (Acts)
1	Both experienced the murmuring of God's people.	'the LORD; for that he heareth your murmurings against the LORD: and what are we, that ye murmur against us ...' (Ex 16.7)	'And in those days ... there arose a murmuring of the Grecians against the Hebrews ...' (6.1)
2	Both contended with a mixed multitude.	'a mixed multitude went up also with them ...' (Ex 12.38)	'the Grecians against the Hebrews ...' (6.1)
3	Both performed mighty miracles.	Deut 34.11	6.8
4	Both were opposed by religious fellow-citizens.	Korah, Dathan & Abiram against Moses (Num 16)	Hellenist Jews confronted Stephen (himself a Hellenist, 6.9)
5	The faces of both men shone.	Ex 34.29	6.15
6	Both experience murderous resistance.	Ex 17.4	6.12; 7.58
7	Both interceded for the nation.	'forgive their sin ... and if not, blot me ... out of thy book' (Ex 32.32)	'Lay not this sin to their charge' (7.60)
8	Before they died, they both saw unique topographies.	Promised Land (Deut 34.1, 4)	heaven (7.56)
9	Both had unique deaths.	Deut 34.5, 6	7.59, 60
10	Both men were followed by unique successors.	Joshua (Deut 34.9)	Saul (7.58)

7

PUBLIC PREACHING AT SAMARIA AND PERSONAL EVANGELISM IN THE DESERT (8.1-40)

STEPHEN'S MARTYRDOM TRIGGERED mass persecution against the early church in Jerusalem (vv1-4). In the chaos that followed, few avoided the havoc wrought by Saul and others. A church that had been richly blessed now experienced severe oppression. Nevertheless, under God's unassailable sovereignty, 'they that were scattered abroad went every where preaching the word' (v4; cf. 14. 22), each believer ultimately being carefully planted in the place where God wanted him to be. Thus, the Lord used their suffering to further His purpose and spread His word. Later, after Saul's conversion, the Lord used conditions of peace to bless His word: 'then had the churches rest … and … multiplied' (9.31). If we can hold on to the truth of God's sovereignty, both in our salvation (cf. 1 Pet 1.2) and our circumstances, we, like these early saints, will be motivated to evangelise regardless of location and conditions.

The spread of the gospel is often a community effort (v4). Although many of these early saints may not have been evangelists *per se* (Eph 4.11), they fulfilled the great commission (Mt 28.19, 20), 'announcing the glad tidings [*euaggelizō*] of the word' (v4, JND). Philip, a gifted evangelist, 'preached [*kēryssō*, announced authoritatively] the Christ' to all of Samaria (v5, JND). He did not rely on social enterprise, worldly innovation, acting, or even charitable works. Instead, because 'faith cometh by hearing, and hearing by the word of God' (Rom 10.17), Philip obeyed Christ's command, 'Go ye into all the world and preach the gospel' (Mk 16.15). The gospel is a message communicated primarily through words. Even though public preaching is currently out of vogue, we must continue to follow the example of these first century Christians and the mandate of Christ Himself.

Even though the Lord Jesus is the *Chief Sower*, He desires His people to share in the work of sowing and reaping (Jn 4.35-38). As He said, 'look on the fields; they are white already to harvest' (Jn 4.35). Sowing God's word is a hard and long-term work requiring diligence. But if we never sow, we will never reap. Furthermore, though we may sow and others water, it is always God Who gives the increase (1 Cor 3.6). During the public ministry of Christ the Samaritan woman had 'left her waterpot, and went her way into the city, and [said]to the men, Come, see a man, which told me all things that ever I did: is not this the Christ' (Jn 4.28 29)? Philip was now another link in the chain of testimony at Samaria, each individual having a part to play.

The spread of the gospel inevitably encounters opposition (vv9-13, 18-23), the root cause being Satan himself, the god of this world, who blinds unbelieving minds (2 Cor 4.4). Just as Stephen faced demonic activity in Samaria (v7), Christians still 'wrestle ... against spiritual wickedness in high places' (Eph 6.12; cf. 2 Cor 10.3, 4).

When spreading the gospel, we may encounter people who do not possess, but merely profess salvation. Simon the sorcerer was such an individual. Whereas the Samaritans believed in the name of Jesus Christ (v12), Simon was more interested in Philip's miracles. Kenneth Wuest translates verse 13 as follows: 'Simon himself also believed and ... continuing as an adherent of Philip, viewing with an interested and critical eye ... the attesting miracles ... which excited wonder as they were being performed, was being rendered beside himself with amazement.'[12] Sadly, as with so many, Simon's profession of faith was merely based on externals. He was not truly resting on Christ (cf. Jn 2.23-25; 4.45).

The fact that Simon never received the Holy Spirit and was strongly rebuked by Peter (vv18-23), shows that he never had saving faith. If there is no fruit of the Spirit, there was never new birth by the Spirit. If there is no change in the life, there was no salvation. 'Faith without works is dead' (James 2.20, 26). Unless a person continues to make his 'calling and election sure' (2 Pet 1.10), the likelihood is he was never saved.

Since this was a new work at the dawn of a new dispensation, it was important for it to have apostolic confirmation (vv14-17). Philip humbly accepted Peter and John's endorsement of his labours. Because jealousy spoils God's work, we must constantly remember we are only slaves in the Master' service – there should be no room for self.

The visible manifestation of the Samaritans receiving the Holy Spirit proved that they were now part of the church, 'where there is neither Greek nor Jew, circumcision nor uncircumcision … but Christ is all, and in all' (Col 3.11). They were by no means inferior to their Jewish brethren, but Christ was supreme. This is the ultimate goal in all our evangelism: Christ glorified and pre-eminent.

DL Moody once said to a critic 'frankly, I sometimes do not like my way of doing evangelism. But I like my way of doing it better than your way of not doing it.' The lesson is simple – go out and preach the word (v25).

Personal evangelism is an important, though often neglected, aspect of gospel outreach. This brief account of Philip's rendezvous with an Ethiopian eunuch illustrates how it should work, God's sovereignty acting in perfect harmony with human efforts to bring sinners to Christ.

During a fruitful gospel campaign in the city of Samaria 'the angel of the Lord spake unto Philip, saying, Arise, and go toward the south unto the way that goeth down from Jerusalem unto Gaza, which is desert' (vv5, 6, 26). Having been 'destroyed by Alexander the Great in the fourth century ... [and then] ... in ... 96 B.C. completely overthrown by the Maccabean prince Alexander ... [Gaza] was literally desert.'[13] It made no sense to travel to a waste land. Why would an evangelist move from a city, with many people, to a desert, with none? Nevertheless, Philip 'arose and went' (v27).

It is only after he recorded Philip's obedience that Luke pointed out, 'behold, a man of Ethiopia, an eunuch of great authority under Candace queen of the Ethiopians, who had the charge of all her treasure, and had come [more than 200 miles] to Jerusalem for to worship, was returning, and sitting in his chariot read Esaias the prophet' (vv27, 28). This man was spiritually disadvantaged in at least three ways. First, as a Gentile, he was an alien 'from the commonwealth of Israel, and [a stranger] from the covenants of promise, having no hope, and without God in the world' (Eph 2.12). Second, being a eunuch, he was barred from entering the congregation of Israel (Deut 23.1). Third, his high-ranking office in the Ethiopian court and probable great personal wealth made it harder for him to receive Christ. 'For it is easier for a camel to go through a needle's eye, than for a rich man to enter into the kingdom of God' (Lk 18.25).

But God had awakened in this Ethiopian eunuch a true desire for Himself (cf. Rom 3.11). In Isaiah's prophecy, Jehovah promised godly Gentiles, 'Even them will I bring to my holy mountain, and make them joyful in my house of prayer: their burnt offerings and their sacrifices *shall be* accepted upon mine altar; for mine house shall be called an house of prayer for all people' (Is 56.7). He assured faithful eunuchs, 'Even unto them will I give in mine house and within my walls a place and a name better than of sons and of daughters' (Is 56.5). In relation to how difficult it is for rich men to enter the kingdom, Christ explained, 'The things which are impossible with men are possible with God' (Lk 18.27). And yet, in the Sermon on the Mount, He urged men to 'seek, and ye shall find' (Mt 7.7). This eunuch sought God. He did not find the solution to his quest at Jerusalem, but God answered his search by means of Isaiah 53 and Philip the evangelist.

Of course, God's timing was perfect. 'Then the Spirit said unto Philip, Go near, and join thyself to this chariot' (v29). Still obedient and not wishing to miss any opportunity to evangelise, 'Philip ran thither to him and heard him read the prophet Esaias, and said, Understandest thou what thou readest?' (v30). The eunuch, humbly pursuing the truth, replied, 'How can I, except some man should guide me? And he desired Philip that he would come up and sit with him' (v31). He had been reading Isaiah chapter 53, which so graphically foresaw Christ's submissive suffering. The Septuagint's reversal of the phrases 'led as a sheep to the slaughter; and like a lamb dumb before his shearer, so opened he not his mouth' (v32), emphasised the barbaric character of the cross as well as the Saviour's perfect self-control. 'When he was reviled, [He] reviled not again; when he suffered, he threatened not' (1 Pet 2.23; cf. Prov 19.11). With an excellent knowledge of God's word, 'Philip opened his mouth, and began at the same scripture, and preached unto him Jesus' (v35).

When the eunuch believed with all his heart 'that Jesus Christ is the Son of God', Philip baptised him (vv36-38). 'And when they were come up out of the water, the Spirit of the Lord caught away Philip, that the eunuch saw him no more' (v39). The evangelist had gone, but because the eunuch now had Christ, he 'went on his way rejoicing' (v39).

We too must be led by the Holy Spirit in our personal evangelism, ever sensitive and obedient to God's guidance (Rom 8.14). 'A man's heart deviseth his way: but the LORD directeth his steps' (Prov

16.9). We should ask the Lord to bring us into contact with people who are genuinely seeking Him and grasp every opportunity to tell others about the Saviour. If individuals confess Christ as Lord, baptism should follow without delay. New converts need discipling, but where this is not possible, as with the eunuch, they may safely be entrusted to the Shepherd and Bishop of souls (1 Pet 2.25). After all, the work is His, not ours.

PART 2

UNTO THE UTTERMOST PART OF THE EARTH
(9.1-21.17)

IN THE OLD TESTAMENT, JEHOVAH GRACIOUSLY chose Israel as His highly prized, special people, set apart from the surrounding nations and devoted entirely to Himself (Ex 19.5; Deut 7.6, 7; 14.2; 26.18, 19). The Law, uniquely given to Israel, was designed to protect her from the idolatrous practices of her Gentile neighbours. The dietary prohibitions alone prevented Israelites from eating with Gentiles (Lev 11). Devout Jews took this one stage further, refusing even to enter a Gentile house (10.28; 11.3). In His atoning death, Christ broke 'down the middle wall of partition *between* [Jew and Gentile]; having abolished in his flesh the enmity, *even* the law of commandments *contained* in ordinances; for to make in himself of twain one new man, *so* making peace' (Eph 2.14, 15). Jews, treated like children under Law (Gal 4.1-3), were 'now to leave their childhood and learn to live and be trusted as grown-up sons. One of the first things to go was the food laws.'[1] The God Who instituted them now annulled them (10.15; 11.9). Everything could now be eaten (cf. 1 Tim 4.3-5). Of course, in His public ministry the Lord Jesus had already 'declared all foods clean' (Mk 7.19, NASB).

But how could the longstanding division between Jews and Gentiles, so clearly laid out in Mosaic Law and firmly embedded in the Jewish conscience, be functionally abolished in the church? The story of Cornelius answers this key question (10.1-11.18). It shows how the doctrinal reality 'that the Gentiles should be fellowheirs, and of the same body, and partakers of His promise in Christ by the gospel' (Eph 3.6), was realised practically. Of course, Luke, being a converted Gentile physician, had great personal interest in this vital issue.

Meanwhile, about the time of Stephen's stoning (which Saul had fully endorsed), severe persecution in Jerusalem led to many believers being 'scattered abroad [*diaspeirō*, to sow throughout] throughout the regions of Judaea and Samaria', some travelling 'as far as Phenice, and Cyprus, and Antioch' (8.1; 11.19). 'Phenice' (11.19; 15.3), also known as 'Phenicia' (21.2), or Phoenicia, was the narrow coastal strip between the Mediterranean and the Lebanon mountain range, now called Lebanon. Christ's own ministry extended into this region (Mt 15.21). Later in Acts we read of at least three churches in this area: at Tyre (21.3, 4), Ptolemais (21.7), and Sidon (27.3). During their first missionary journey, Barnabas and Saul preached on the island of Cyprus (13.4-13). Antioch, capital city of the Roman province of Syria, was the third largest city in the Empire (after Rome and Alexandria), with an estimated population of 500,000.[2] At first, the scattered disciples preached 'the word to none but unto the Jews only' (11.19). But things changed. When several from Cyprus and Cyrene ('a Greek colonial city in North Africa,'[3] cf. Mt 27.32), arrived in Antioch, they 'spoke to the Hellenists also, preaching the Lord Jesus. And the hand of the Lord was with them, and a great number who believed turned to the Lord' (11.20, 21, ESV). As far as the Acts record is concerned, this was 'the first church to be planted outside of Jerusalem and Judaea.[4]

When 'tidings of these things came unto the ears of the church which was in Jerusalem … they sent forth Barnabas, that he should go as far as Antioch' (11.22). Their delegate choice proved crucial to the work of God. Although Barnabas, being a Cypriot Levite (4.36), came from a dispersion family, he 'was regarded with complete confidence in Jerusalem and acted as a pivot or link between the Hebrew and Hellenistic elements in the church.'[5] Being 'full of the Holy Ghost and of faith', and the only man in Acts to be called 'good', Barnabas was exceptionally godly (11.24). As a natural encourager (4.36; cf. 9.27), sensitive and discerning, 'when he came, and had seen the grace of God, [he] was glad' (v23). Avoiding any attempt to impose Mosaic Law on these newly converted Gentiles, he 'exhorted them all, that with purpose of heart they would cleave unto the Lord' (11.23).

Appreciating his own limitations, while understanding the enormity of the task in hand, Barnabas departed 'to Tarsus, for to seek Saul' (11.25). Tarsus, a university city in the imperial province of Cilicia, was 'ranked as a free city under the Romans from 64 B.C.'[6] Three years post-conversion, after a brief visit to Jerusalem, Saul had returned to Tarsus, his home city (9.28-30; Gal 1.18, 21). When Barnabas found him, he was likely obeying his divine call and evangelising the Gentile 'regions of Syria and Cilicia' (9.15; Gal 2.2). The churches of 'Syria and Cilicia', which he strengthened at the beginning of his second missionary journey, had probably been founded during this initial preaching period (15.41).

Saul responded positively to Barnabas' request. 'And when he had found him, he brought him unto Antioch. And it came to pass, that a whole year they assembled themselves with the church, and taught much people. And the disciples were called Christians first in Antioch' (11.26). Their one year of teaching together shows the priority local churches should give to Christ-exalting Bible exposition, the need for new believers to be established in the faith, and the benefit of sitting under the varied ministry of more than one teacher.

When the Jerusalem-based prophet Agabus came to Antioch, he 'signified by the Spirit that there should be great dearth throughout all the world: which came to pass in the days of Claudius Caesar' (v28). Moved with pity for their Jewish brethren, these Gentile Christians, 'every man according to his ability, determined to send relief unto the brethren which dwelt in Judaea: which also they did, and sent it to the elders by the hands of Barnabas and Saul' (vv29, 30). Such generosity must have contributed to the practical fusion of Christian Jews and Gentiles. After delivering the gift, Paul and

Barnabas returned from Jerusalem to Antioch, accompanied now by John Mark (12.25).

During the first missionary journey, after leaving Cyprus, John Mark 'returned to Jerusalem' (13.13), something which caused trouble later (15.36-41). Sadly, the fellowship between Jerusalem and Antioch temporarily soured when men from Judaea told the Antioch Christians they had to be circumcised and keep the Law of Moses (15.1). This prompted the Jerusalem council, which further addressed the issue of Gentile Christians being accepted by their Jewish brothers (15.2-31).

8

SAUL'S CONVERSION AND PETER'S MINISTRY (9.1-43)

In chapters 1 – 7, God had reached out time and again to Israel (the sons of Shem). Sadly, Jewish history repeated itself. Just as their fathers had resisted God in the wilderness, this current generation had hardened their hearts against the Son of God during His time among them, and now post-Pentecost steadfastly resisted the Holy Spirit (7.51). Because they utterly rejected the Triune God, 'blindness in part ... happened to Israel' (Rom 11.25). The stoning of Stephen signalled a change in God's dealings with the Semitic people-group. The salvation of the Ethiopian eunuch (a son of Ham, chapter 8) showed that the gospel was going global.

When the Lord Jesus personally commissioned Saul of Tarsus on the road to Damascus to preach to the Gentiles, He showed His desire for the sons of Japheth to be reached with the gospel (26.17). This 'Hebrew of the Hebrews' (Phil 3.5), with outstanding Jewish credentials, would serve among Gentile 'dogs' (cf. Mt 15.22-28). God's ways are infinitely higher than ours. He uses whom He chooses. As sovereign Lord, He changed this persecutor into a mighty preacher of the gospel. Having been chosen in eternity in Christ (Eph 1.4) to salvation (2 Thess 2.13) and to testify of God's saving grace, Saul was an elect vessel (9.15), separated from his mother's womb for the purpose of God (Gal 1.15). Our experience is the same: by sovereign grace alone elect, saved and serving. Praise His name. The Shem, Ham and Japheth structure of Acts proves God 'will have all men to be saved' (1 Tim 2.4).

A pattern

Just as the God of glory (7.2) appeared to Abraham in the midst of heathen darkness, so 'the glory of God in the face of Jesus Christ' (2 Cor 4.6) burst upon the horizon of Saul's religious darkness. Although his conversion only occupies a few verses in chapter 9, he recounted it with increasing intensity and thankfulness. We first read that 'there shined around about him a light from heaven' (9.3). Saul later described it as 'a great light' (22.6), and, finally, as 'a light … above the brightness of the sun' (26.13). This chief of sinners never forgot the sublime joy of being saved. Neither should we. Like Saul, we should constantly wonder at and be thankful for our own salvation.

Saul left Jerusalem intent on bringing back Christians as captives; instead, after the Lord appeared to him, he was led by the hand as Christ's captive. On the road to Damascus, Saul learnt the revolutionary idea that Jesus Christ is Lord. He immediately understood that the voice and glory from heaven was God's: 'who art thou, Lord' (9.5)? It was earthshattering to hear God say 'I am Jesus' (9.5). Jesus of Nazareth was not the pseudo-Messiah, self-styled redeemer, that Saul had thought, but the divine Lord. Heretofore, Saul had, in ignorant unbelief, persecuted the name of Jesus, convinced that his followers were idolatrous, heretical apostates. He now learnt what every new convert understands: that Jesus Christ is the Son of God.

The Lord's response to the apostle, 'I am Jesus whom thou persecutest' (9.5), teaches vital doctrines. Persecuting the church in ignorance and unbelief (1 Tim 1.13), he likely swallowed the conspiracy theory that the disciples had stolen the body (Mt 28.15). For the first time he understood the indisputable fact of the bodily resurrection of Christ, and his subsequent ascension. By revelation, here in embryonic form, he began to appreciate the mystery of the church, the body of Christ (Eph 1.22-23; 3.3, 6). It was fitting, at the outset of a new dispensation, that divine secrets, hidden for so long, should be revealed to the apostle of the Gentiles. He had ignorantly persecuted a company in vital and living union with the risen Christ; with the same zeal, now redirected, he would tirelessly make known the wonder of the church being the body and the bride of Christ. May we never cease to marvel at the truth; 'in Christ Jesus ye who sometimes were far off are made nigh by the blood of Christ' (Eph 2.13).

The words, 'it is hard for thee to kick against the pricks' (9.5), emphasise the truth that God is longsuffering and not willing that any should perish. Saul became a textbook convert, a prototype of sorts (1 Tim 1.16). Every subsequent conversion would follow a similar pattern: conviction of sin, a pricked conscience, the recognition of guilt, and a final reliance on Christ. To varying degrees every conversion has followed this Pauline model. In a day when Satan makes false professors and sows counterfeit Christians, we must remember what happened to Saul of Tarsus, the pattern convert. Easy believism and an absence of fruit after profession violate Saul's conversion pattern. James is very forthright: 'faith without works is dead' (James 2.20).

Having seen the risen Lord, Saul fell to the earth, completely humbled; and for three days and three nights did not eat nor drink. The fear, awe, and wonder of beholding the Lord's glory stripped him of every worldly and material desire. May we also be blind to what is temporal and fleeting, fixing our eyes upon the risen Man in glory.

A pattern for living

Paul was also a template for Christian living (1 Cor 11.1). While he experienced some extraordinary events which Christians today will never experience, much of Paul's life was marked by the ordinary disciplines of the Christian life. After conversion, he relied on revelation from God for direction. In this instance, he received an open vision, although in later life he read the word of God written on parchment. We today are equally reliant on revelation from heaven, not through visions but via the closed canon of Scripture. Further, Saul prayed, a discipline which no Christian outgrows. As soon as he was able, Saul was baptised, as every Christian should be. We will never reach the stage where we are too spiritual to read God's word, to pray and live in the good of our baptism – dying to self and sin. Let us seek to follow Paul as he followed Christ.

Although Saul became the last of the apostles, even this great man needed other Christians as he brought the gospel to the Gentiles. The remainder of the chapter shows him dependent on Ananias, the disciples at Damascus, Barnabas, the assembly at Jerusalem, and the apostle Peter to fulfil his commission. Had he not worked in harmony with them, he would not have been able to function. Neither can we achieve much without the help of others. Ananias was the first to embrace Saul as a brother and encourage him in the faith. Babes in Christ can be stumbled and stifled without due care, but under the wise tutelage of mature saints (no matter how brief) they can flourish.

Saul speedily associated himself with people of like mind; for example, he was 'with the disciples ... at Damascus' (9.19). Growing in grace, he loved to preach Christ and exercise the spiritual gifts given to him. His burning desire to make Christ known should rebuke our apathy. The period described as 'many days' (9.23), encompass his preaching work but also refer to his time in Arabia (Gal 1.17). These years are hidden from us, but exemplify the principle that the servant of God must spend time in secret with the Lord, and wait on Him. The Damascus disciples, with him in the good times, helped him through the difficult days of persecution, enabling him to escape in a basket. In this way, through thick and thin, they exemplified Christian unity.

Everywhere Saul went he made every effort to fellowship with the Lord's people (9.26). The caution exercised by the believers at Jerusalem on the issue of reception is highly commendable. Ultimately, however, they received him on the commendation of Barnabas, who knew his manner of life. Whilst caution needs to be exercised in the matter of assembly reception, we must avoid adding extra-biblical requirements which simply reflect our own biases.

Saul made the assembly the centre of all he did. 'Coming in and going out' (9.28) with a local company of believers, he was in fellowship with them in the full sense of the word, exercising the gifts given to him by the Triune God. May we throw our all into the house of God because what we build into it will last for all eternity (1 Cor 3.13). Jerusalem was not, however, to be Saul's base of operations. With the aid of the local believers, the Lord sent him to Troas. May the Lord help us to labour in the locality where he has placed us, knowing we are there according to His sovereign prerogative.

Peter

Saul, however, did not have a monopoly on gospel preaching. Having heard little of Peter since chapter 6, we now see this mighty apostle emulating Christ's miracles, with many on the west coast of Israel turning to the Lord (9.35, 42).

Dorcas had laid some of the groundwork in Joppa for gospel testimony. While she was not a public preacher, her loving labours and good works helped local people see Christ in her. Although a social gospel has no place in Holy writ, believers should endeavour to get to know and bear testimony to the people in their locality.

Although the gospel is a verbal message, it is supported by the witness of godly lives. This is what we see in Dorcas.

Peter stayed a while in Joppa . We do not read of Saul in earnest until chapter 13. Again, we learn that gospel work involves many inter-connected Christians labouring together. Although Paul was the apostle to the Gentiles, the Lord was going to use Peter first in Joppa to open the door of faith to the Gentiles through Cornelius. Paul would then use this foundation to preach to Japheth's other sons in Europe. God was sovereignly working out His gospel plan in a way that involved every believer. They were of one spirit and one mind 'striving together for the faith of the gospel' (Phil 1.27). May we follow their example for the glory of the Lord.

9

CORNELIUS (10.1-11.18)

The story of Cornelius answers two critical questions. First, how did God practically dissolve the divide between Jewish and Gentile believers? Second, how did He respond to a genuinely seeking Gentile sinner?

Cornelius' angelic visitation (10.1-8, 22, 30-33; 11.13, 14)

The professional soldier Cornelius was 'a devout man', God-fearing and 'just' (10.1, 2, 22). Generous and prayerful, he was highly respected by local Jews (10.2, 22) and noticed by God. Like Old Testament ascending (Lev 1.3) or grain offerings (of which a 'memorial' was burnt on the altar, Lev 2.2), Cornelius' prayers and alms came 'up for a memorial before God' (10.4). But those Old Testament sacrifices could never save; neither could Cornelius' devotions. Sensing this, he prayed for more light. God answered him in the same way He answered Daniel's prayers, using an angelic visitation (10.31; cf. Dan 8.15; 9.3, 20-22).

At the ninth hour (3 pm), while Cornelius fasted and prayed, a holy angel, in the form of a man dressed 'in bright clothing', entered his house, stood before him, and addressed him by name (10.3, 22, 30; 11.13). The vision was clear ('evidently' translates *phonerōs*, meaning plainly), gripping ('looked' translates *atenizō*, to gaze intently), and terrifying ('he was afraid') (10.3, 4). When Cornelius asked, 'What is it, Lord?' (10.4), the angel instructed him to send 'to Joppa, and call hither Simon, whose surname is Peter; he is lodged in the house of one Simon a tanner by the sea side ... who shall tell thee words, whereby thou and all thy house shall be saved' (10.5, 6, 22, 32; 11.13, 14). Staying with a tanner may indicate 'that the strictness of the Jewish law was losing its hold on Peter; since the tanner's occupation was regarded as unclean by strict Jews, and the tanners were commanded to dwell alone'. As soon as the angel departed, Cornelius 'called two of his household servants, and a devout soldier of them that waited on him continually; and when he had declared all these things unto them, he sent them to Joppa' (vv7, 8).

Peter's heavenly vision (10.7-23, 28; 11.4-12)

God works in harmony with our prayers. As Cornelius' messengers 'drew nigh unto the city, Peter went up upon the housetop to pray about the sixth hour [12 pm]' (10.9; cf. Ps 55.17; Dan 6.10). Weakened with hunger, undistracted by others, and falling 'into a trance', he saw a 'vision' of 'heaven opened, and a certain vessel descending unto him, as it had been a great sheet knit at the four corners … wherein were all manner of four footed beasts of the earth, and wild beasts, and creeping things [*herpeton*, reptiles], and fowls of the air' (10.10-12, 17, 19; 11.5, 6; cf. Gen 1.25; 6.20; Rom 1.23). The Greek word translated 'corners' 'was a technical expression … for the ends of a bandage.'[8] This wide range of creatures represented every major group of land-based animals and birds, probably mixing the ceremonially clean and unclean (Lev 11). Having been 'let down from heaven', this great sheet was then 'received up again' (10.16; 11.5, 10).

A heavenly voice commanded Peter to 'kill, and eat' (10.13; 11.7). Despite his hunger (which heightened the effectiveness of the vision), Peter responded, 'Not so, Lord; for I have never eaten any thing that is common or unclean' (10.14; 11.8). It was like Ezekiel's reaction when told to eat cakes baked with human excrement (Eze

4.9-14). Having observed Jewish dietary restrictions from birth, Peter was horrified by the thought of eating ceremonially unclean flesh. While God permitted Ezekiel to replace human faeces with 'cow's dung' (Eze 4.15), Peter was given no such concession. A greater issue was at stake – church unity. God, the Maker of all (Gen 1.24), gave every creature to Noah for food (Gen 9.3). Although temporarily limiting the animals Israel could eat, He now removed such dietary restrictions. 'What God hath cleansed, that call not thou common' (10.15). So important was the message, Peter was given the vision three times (10.16; 11.10).

Having 'fastened [his] eyes [*atenizō*, to gaze intently]' upon and 'considered' what he saw (11.6), Peter was 'greatly perplexed' (10.17, NASB). 'And while Peter was reflecting on the vision, the Spirit said unto him, Behold, three men are looking for you. But arise, go downstairs, and accompany them without misgivings; for I have sent them Myself' (vv19, 20; 11.11, 12, NASB). Their perfectly timed arrival and message, the vision, the heavenly voice, and the Spirit's prompting, all clinched the lesson in Peter's mind. If he should no longer deem any animal unclean, how could he view Gentiles as unclean, who ate these animals? That night Peter lodged the three Gentile messengers; the next day, 'without raising any objection', he travelled with them from Joppa to Caesarea, accompanied by six Jewish brethren (10.23, 29; 11.12, NASB). Ironically, it was to Joppa that Jonah fled to avoid preaching to Gentile Nineveh (Jonah 1.3).

Peter's gospel message (10.24-48; 11.12-17; 15.17-9)

Arriving at Caesarea, Peter did something which, as an orthodox Jew, he would never have done before. He entered a Gentile house (10.24, 28; 11.12). There, he found Cornelius, his kinsmen, and near friends eagerly waiting (10.24, 27). In his enthusiasm, Cornelius 'fell down at [Peter's] feet, and worshipped him' (10.25). Of course, Peter immediately corrected this misplaced veneration, taking 'him up, [and] saying, Stand up; I myself also am a man' (10.26; cf. 14.11-18; Rev 19.10; 22.8, 9). With candour, Peter explained that although it was 'an unlawful thing for a man that is a Jew to keep company, or come unto one of another nation … God hath shewed me that I should not call any man common or unclean … I ask therefore for what intent ye have sent for me' (10.28, 29). Cornelius, in turn, recounted his angelic visitation three days previously and clarified that everyone was 'present before God, to hear all things that are commanded thee of God' (10.30-33; 11.13, 14).

Having established that, as far as salvation is concerned, Jews and Gentiles were on a level playing field (10.34, 35), Peter preached a four-phased, theocentric, Christ-exalting message (10.36-43). Phase 1: the Old Testament **anticipated** Christ, bearing 'witness, that through his name whosoever believeth in him shall receive remission of sins' (10.43). Phase 2: John the Baptist **announced** Christ (10.37). Phase 3: fulfilling prophecy, 'God **anointed** Jesus of Nazareth with the Holy Ghost and with power' (10.38; cf. Is 61.1; Lk 4.18). This anointing, which took place at His baptism, inaugurated a public ministry (witnessed by the apostles) of 'preaching peace … doing good, and healing all that were oppressed of the devil; for God was with him' (10.36, 38, 39). Unlike secular rulers, who described themselves as 'benefactors' (Lk 22.25), or even Cornelius, who did many good works, Peter presented for 'admiration and faith the supreme doer of good.'[9] The Lord's ministry had a generally southward direction of travel, beginning in Galilee and ending in Jerusalem. It was here the Jews crucified Him, so completing His public service (10.39; cf. 1.21, 22). Even though Christ preached primarily 'unto the children of Israel', His fame had spread widely (10.36,37). Phase 4: God **appointed** Jesus of Nazareth to be 'Judge of the living and the dead' (10.42, NASB). He confirmed this appointment by raising Him from the dead and showing Him openly to preselected witnesses, who ate and drank with Him (10.40, 41; 17.31). The Lord then commanded His disciples 'to preach unto the people' (10.42). This final phase was mostly in a northward, moving away from Jerusalem (1.8).

As soon as Cornelius and his friends heard the gospel, they believed it, God 'purifying their hearts by faith'; as a result, the Holy Spirit came and indwelt them (10.44-47; 11.15, 17; 15.7-9). When they spoke (supernaturally) in foreign languages and magnified God, Peter and the six Hebrew Christians accompanying him were 'astonished', for God had given saved Gentiles the same 'gift of the Holy Ghost' (10.45) as He had to Jewish disciples at Pentecost ('at the beginning', 11.15). Remembering the Saviour's pre-ascension prediction of Spirit baptism and feeling unable to 'withstand God', Peter 'commanded them to be baptized in the name of the Lord. Then prayed they him to tarry certain days' (1.5; 10.48; 11.16, 17).

Peter's successful defence (11.1-18)

This section is bookended by the subsequent reaction of the Jerusalem-based apostles and brethren. First, they 'heard that the Gentiles had also received the word of God' (v1). When Peter came to Jerusalem they challenged him, 'saying, Thou wentest in to men uncircumcised, and didst eat with them' (vv2, 3). But, having 'heard' his compelling, comprehensive, and orderly exposition of the entire series of events, 'they held their peace, and glorified God' (v18).

10

PETER'S DELIVERANCE AND HEROD'S DEATH (12.1-25)

THIS CHAPTER VIVIDLY DEMONSTRATES how God may bring His people through wave after wave of trouble, even though He has the power to stop it. While the Judean believers were suffering a **famine** (11.27-30), 'at that time' Herod began his malicious **persecution** which resulted in James' execution. Had God not intervened, Peter would have died too. Their contrasting fates show that God could have saved James if He had chosen to. Since He didn't, He evidently had a purpose in James' death. By the same token, He must have had a purpose in the famine (Paul saw one, Rom 15.25-27). Even though we may not perceive it, we may be sure God has a design in His people's sufferings today (Rom 8.28).

Herod's display of power (vv1-3)

Herod's actions revealed a man in love with power. When he 'stretched forth his hands' (v1), things happened. James could not escape him (v2) – so much for the Christian's God! The Jews liked the spectacle of violence against Christians, so Herod intended to indulge them further (v3). Using the military power at his disposal he had Peter 'apprehended' and heavily guarded – all with a view to providing a Passover time display for the Jews (v4). The timing is reminiscent of the Lord's treatment at the hands of wicked men.

Deliberately set against this impressive demonstration of power is the picture of apparent weakness: a church that can do nothing but pray (v5). And how they prayed! The whole story pivots on this point. Herod had planned to maximise his popularity with the

Jews, but God would turn the tables into a humiliation of greater measure. Herod was about to learn what the Lord told Pilate: 'thou couldest have no power at all against me, except it were given thee from above' (Jn 19.11). God allows proud man to go so far, but, like the sea waves, there is a point at which He says, 'thus far and no further' (Job 38.8-11).

Peter's miraculous escape (vv4-11)

The divine intervention resulting in Peter's release from prison underlines important principles about biblical miracles. Firstly, **miracles are not naturally explicable.** They involve the temporary alteration of the rules by which God normally governs the universe. In this instance, Peter's two chains falling from his hands defies the expected behaviour of metallic artefacts. In addition, Peter's walk, undetected, past a high security guard defies the normal behaviour of guards – bear in mind Roman soldiers risked <u>fustuarium</u> (being beaten to death) for sleeping on duty. The fact that the escape remained undetected till morning suggests a trance or sleep came upon them. And then there is the iron gate automatically swinging open (v10). This defies normal laws of motion – no visible force was applied to it, yet it opened. Put these elements together and we are left with a choice: the story is fabricated or it is miraculous. We come to the same point as we read through the word of God and as we investigate the person of Christ (Jn 20.30-31). It is impossible to accept the Bible as God's word yet strip it of the supernatural. After all, what is incredible about the Creator occasionally intervening in His world?

Secondly, **miracles are not normally expected**. In Acts 12 we are in the period and with the people through whom God was performing miracles, designed to validate the apostolic preaching (Heb 2.3-4). Yet when Peter was released, the saints were 'astonished' (v16). This is no criticism, for James had just been executed. Miraculous intervention then, is God's prerogative, but He is under no obligation to do so to satisfy the whim of man (Mt 27.40; Lk 16.31).

Thirdly, **miracles are not needlessly employed**. Just look at what Peter had to do for himself. He had to get up, dress, put on his sandals, follow the angel on foot, and then, when the angel left him one street away from the prison, use his initiative. Angels serve 'them who shall be heirs of salvation' (Heb 1.14), but clearly, they don't do for saints what saints can do for themselves – a guiding principle to bear in mind when seeking to help saints in need.

The engine room of the church (vv12-17)

A positive effect of the adverse situation was that it **united** 'the church' in prayer (v5). The scene in Mary's house where 'many were praying' is heart-warming. Rhoda answering the door shows the saints felt at home there. Imagine sitting as a first-time visitor in someone's house and hearing the front door being knocked. On the first visit it may feel that it is not your place to greet visitors, you are a visitor yourself. But now imagine being in a house you have often frequented. The homeowner knows you well, and treats you like one of the family. To be asked to answer the door, or to simply answer it unasked, is perfectly natural. (v13). But best of all, the saints felt free to pray there. The whole church may not have been able to attend the late-night emergency prayer meeting, but their contribution to the prayer effort from elsewhere was still registered and it still availed. Their prayer was **fervent,** being offered 'without ceasing' (v5), a word which according to Vine means 'to stretch out'. They certainly stretched themselves, continuing in prayer well into the night, past Peter's bedtime at least (v6).

As to the content of their prayer, the only clue we have is that it was 'for him' (v5), i.e., for Peter. The incident therefore encourages **intercessory** prayer. We may conclude their prayer was **effective** by looking at what followed it, and thus find guidance when praying for those in need today. First, *Peter was sleeping*. The expectation of his execution was at fever pitch, and he was in the most uncomfortable of beds – doubly chained between two soldiers (v6) – yet he was sleeping so heavily that the angel had to smite him to awaken him (v7). Rest comes from God (Ps 127.2); thus, it is fitting to pray for practical peace for saints experiencing trouble (Jn 16.33). Second, *Peter was set free*. This was entirely at God's discretion, as evidenced by James' execution. Thus we can pray for deliverance from adversity, provided we add the caveat, 'if the Lord will.' Thirdly, *Herod was stopped*. We may bring the threatening of wicked men before God, leaving Him to intervene according to His wisdom (4.29; Dan 2.12-19; Ps 76.10). Fourth, *the saints were surprised*. There is comedy in Rhoda's response – leaving Peter outside while reporting the good news of his release to those in the prayer meeting. But it simply serves to illustrate that God 'is able to do exceeding abundantly above all that we ask or think' (Eph 3.20). Peter made a point of informing them of his release before quickly departing, reminding us that it's important to share answered prayer with those we know are interceding for us.

Herod's demise (vv18-23)

Herod's reaction to the situation has all the hallmarks of wounded pride. First, and understandably, he held the soldiers to public account for Peter's escape by having them executed. How solemn that 16 soldiers lost their lives, ultimately because of their wicked ruler's political whim. Second, Herod moved from Judea to Caesarea. It is reminiscent of Ahithophel who, suffering loss of face, could not continue in the same place, and resorted to suicide (2 Sam

17.23). Herod's pride led directly to his ruin. He was flattered into an insincere reconciliation with the people of Tyre and Sidon and his failure to resist their blasphemous praise resulted in the angel of the Lord smiting for the second time in the chapter, not now to waken Peter (v7) but to execute Herod (v23). His shameful demise illustrates Hebrews 10.31: it is 'a fearful thing to fall into the hands of the living God.'

The enduring resources of the church (vv24, 25)

The chapter ends by drawing a contrast between Herod's demise and the growth of God's word (v24). Proud Herod's intentions had ultimately been frustrated, yet, despite the outward turbulence, God's agenda had quietly moved forward. What had the young church learned? For one thing, their continuation depended not on James, whom Herod killed, nor on Peter, for after his miraculous release from prison Peter had to depart to another place (v17). No matter the usefulness of a human servant, the ultimate resources for the church, then, and now, are 'God, and the word of His grace' (vv5, 24; 20.32). God taught them the lesson by means of a famine, a death, a dramatically averted execution, and the solemn removal of a violent opponent. His lessons are perfectly crafted, at times costly, yet He works all things together after the counsel of His own will – harnessing things created, both fallen and redeemed – to manifest His glory.

11

PAUL'S FIRST MISSIONARY JOURNEY (13, 14)

PAUL'S TRAILBLAZING FIRST MISSIONARY JOURNEY into Cyprus and modern-day Turkey established a biblical pattern for evangelists. Knowing the strength of Christian fellowship, the Holy Spirit called Paul and Barnabas to do this great work together. He then directed it (13.2, 4, 9). The journey, which mostly consisted of pioneering evangelism, began with a commendation from the local church in Antioch.

Conscious of its power, Paul preached 'the word of God' (13.5, 7, 44, 46, 48, 49; 14.3, 25; cf. Heb 4.12). He offered the gospel first in the Jewish synagogues, reflecting a deep love for his own people and a desire for their salvation (Rom 9.1-3; 10.1). It also demonstrated his practical wisdom, for there he found a ready audience, of both Jews and God-fearing Gentiles (13.16, 42, 43). Once the Jews rejected the message, mostly out of envy, he turned to the Gentiles (13.45, 46; cf. 17.5; 18.6); thereafter, when opposition heightened and turned violent, he moved on (13.51; 14.19, 20). Through his preaching, 'as many as were ordained to eternal life believed' (13.48; cf. 18.11). Where new assemblies had been formed through local conversions, Paul endeavoured later to revisit them, 'confirming [*epistērizō*, 'to give additional strength'[10]] the souls of the disciples, and exhorting them to continue in the faith' (14.22). Having appointed elders and 'commended them to the Lord, on whom they believed' (14.23), he left them to continue by themselves. Of course, while physically absent, his earnest prayers and care for them continued.

Even today, evangelism is best done in partnership with other believers, in the Spirit's energy, and with the blessing of a local church. Christians should always seek fresh opportunities to reach out to new areas and new people. Preaching 'the word of God' remains the cornerstone of all evangelism. Although many believers lack the opportunity to preach to Jews, the principle of reaching out to those with whom they have an immediate affinity remains. Christian servants will continue to be opposed but, like Paul, must be 'stedfast, unmoveable, always abounding in the work of the Lord' (1 Cor 15.58). God still oversees all gospel efforts, ensuring that 'as many as were ordained to eternal life' believe. For individual converts and newly established churches there needs to be a healthy balance between encouragement and letting them stand on their own two feet.

Having at least five prophets and teachers of different temperaments, classes and backgrounds, the church at Antioch was exceptionally privileged. Tender-hearted and encouraging, Barnabas was a Cypriot Levite (4.36). Being 'called Niger', Simeon was probably of African extraction. Lucius hailed from Cyrene, a North African port with an established Jewish community.[11] Manaen 'had been brought up with Herod the tetrarch'. Listed last was Saul of Tarsus, a fiercely intelligent, intensely zealous, converted Pharisee (cf. Phil 3.4-6). This international representation reflected the early spread of Christianity and the intended harmony between Jews and Gentiles. For example, at Jerusalem on the Day of Pentecost there were devout Jews from 'the parts of Libya about Cyrene' (2.10). Following 'the persecution that arose about' Stephen's death, some Cypriot and Cyrenian believers escaped to Syrian Antioch, where they preached 'the Lord Jesus' to Gentiles (11.19, 20).

In the absence of a complete Old Testament, prophets spoke directly on God's behalf, unfolding doctrine which had not yet been recorded in written form. Teachers did as they do today, expounding with clarity the sacred text. Even though a finalised canon of Scripture rendered the foundational gift of prophecy unnecessary, the principle remains that local churches should have a plurality of teachers, working together to edify the saints (1 Cor 13.8; 14.19, 26, 29; Eph 2.20). Such Bible-teaching ministry is not prestigious, but a lowly service for Christ, demanding high levels of commitment and self-denial.

As these prophets and teachers at Antioch 'ministered to the Lord, and fasted, the Holy Ghost [probably through one of the prophets] said, Separate Me Barnabas and Saul for the work whereunto I have called them' (13.2). Chosen and called by the Holy Spirit to a work He had planned for them, Barnabas and Saul did not join a missionary society or appeal for financial support. Neither did the church at Antioch arrange a series of committee meetings. Rather, having simply 'fasted and prayed, and laid their hands on them [by way of identification], they sent them away [*apoluō*, 'to free fully']' (v3). Such unassuming commendation, without fanfare, should characterise the beginning of every missionary endeavour. Those considering missionary work should similarly wait on the Spirit's guidance (Rom 8.14), while throwing themselves into the service of their local church.

Cyprus

After travelling to the fortified seaport of Seleucia, Barnabas and Saul sailed to Cyprus, where the gospel had already been preached (11.19). Having come under senatorial rule in BC 22, Cyprus was governed by a proconsul, Sergius Paulus (13.7). Two of its cities, Salamis and Paphos, were renowned devotees of the goddess Paphian, 'a deity of Syrian origin identified with the Greek Aphrodite.[12] The eastern city of Salamis possessed several Jewish synagogues where the missionaries first 'preached the word of God' (v5).

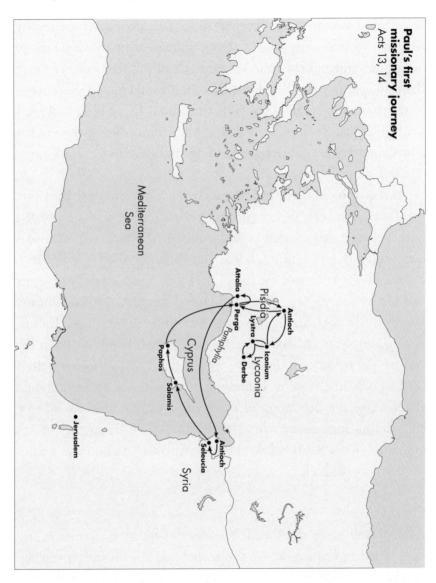

Barnabas came from Cyprus (4.36), and throughout their time on the island his nephew, John Mark, helped the two missionaries (13.5; cf. Col 4.10). But Mark's first foray into missionary work was short lived and soon after leaving Cyprus 'John departing from them returned to Jerusalem' (13.13). No reason is given for his

100

impromptu exit, which eventually contributed to a longstanding rift between Paul and Barnabas (15.37-39). Whatever the cause, Mark recovered sufficiently to write the Gospel of Jehovah's unerring Servant and to be acknowledged by Paul for his usefulness (2 Tim 4.11). Recovery is always possible, and we should never write off another believer.

During his Cyprus narrative Luke permanently switches from the name 'Saul' to 'Paul' (13.9). Here also he begins to chart Paul's rising prominence in the missionary partnership. By the time they reach Antioch, their order has fully reversed from 'Barnabas and Saul' (v2), to 'Paul and Barnabas' (v43). Having said this, Luke's main focus at Cyprus is the intense opposition they faced in the city of Paphos, together with the suddenness and strength of the divine response to the opposition, which prompted the proconsul's conversion.

A Jewish false prophet who dabbled in the occult (v6), Barjesus was the kind of man Isaiah warned Judah against and who, under Mosaic Law, would have been executed (Deut 13.1-5; Is 8.19). The punishment he received was mild in comparison. 'Elymas' was probably not a second name so much as a Semitic word meaning 'sorcerer'[13] (13.6, 8). Even though Barjesus had wormed his way into the centre of power on the island, unconvinced by his craftiness, Sergius Paulus, 'a prudent man … called for Barnabas and Saul, and desired to hear the word of God' (v7).

Probably afraid of losing his influential position, Barjesus 'withstood them, seeking to turn away the deputy from the faith' (v8). Paul reacted with frightening intensity. Filled with the Holy Spirit, he 'set his eyes on him', exposed his wickedness, and, with apostolic authority, pronounced his judgment. Although his name meant 'son of Jesus', he was in reality 'full of all deceit and all craft: son of [the] devil, enemy of all righteousness' (v10, JND). In his wickedness he had attempted to 'pervert [*diastepho*: 'to distort, twist'[14]] the right [*euthus*, 'straight'] ways of the Lord' (v10). He was immediately though temporarily blinded by 'the hand of the Lord' so that 'there fell on him a mist and a darkness' (v11). The man who had sought to turn the deputy from the faith now sought 'some to lead him by the hand' (v11). Deeply impressed by the miracle, Sergius Paulus 'believed, being astonished at the doctrine of the Lord' (v12; Rom 10.17).

As an apostate Jew, Barjesus represented Israel as a whole. His opposition to the gospel was punished by a reversible judicial blindness. Paul explained to the Romans 'that blindness in part is happened to Israel, until the fulness of the Gentiles be come in. And so all Israel shall be saved: as it is written, There shall come out of Sion the Deliverer, and shall turn away ungodliness from Jacob' (Rom 11.25, 26; cf. Is 6.9, 10; Acts 28.26, 27). In the meantime, while we await Israel's national salvation, just as the Gentile Sergius Paulus 'desired to hear the word of God' and 'believed' it (vv7, 12), the gospel is offered to Gentiles.

Antioch

The Roman colony of Antioch was probably founded by Antiochus I Soter in the third century B.C. It now lies in ruins, one kilometre north of modern day Yalvac.[15] Perga is also in ruins, situated fifteen kilometres east of the modern coastal city of Antalya (biblical Attalia, 14.25). The direct two-hundred-kilometre route from Perga to Antioch takes approximately forty hours to walk, which includes a one-thousand metre ascent through the Taurus Mountains. It is more likely that Paul travelled the less arduous and less direct *Via Sebaste*, a Roman road linking Perga with Antioch and other Roman colonies in the area, including Iconium and Lystra.[16]

True to their missionary practice of preaching to the Jews first,

Paul and Barnabas entered the Antioch 'synagogue on the sabbath day, and sat down' (13.14). After the public reading of the Law and the Prophets, invited to give a 'word of exhortation for the people,' Paul stood up and, energetically beckoning with his hand, said, 'Men of Israel, and ye that fear God, give audience' (vv15, 16). In his first recorded sermon we see the results of a lifetime immersed in Old Testament Scripture, coupled with direct revelation from the ascended Christ (Gal 1.12). Paul spoke clearly, concisely, and faithfully, exposing the murderous ignorance of Israel's leaders (v27). His carefully structured message, offering a selective synopsis of Old Testament history (vv17-22) up to the seed of David (vv23-25), drove home the full soteriological implications of the gospel (vv26-39), ending with a stern warning (vv40, 41).

Paul summarised God's gracious ways with the Jewish nation, from the call of the patriarchs to the enthronement of King David and the raising up of his seed (vv17-25). God **chose** Abraham and his family to be His channel of blessing to the world (v17; Gen 12.2). While they were in Egypt under severe persecution, God 'exalted the people' so that 'the more [the Egyptians] afflicted them, the more they multiplied and grew' (v17; Ex 1.12). After four hundred years of affliction, God **delivered** them 'with an high arm' (v17; Gen 15.13; Ex 6.6; Acts 7.6-7), and for the next forty years, as a tender Father, 'nursed them in the desert' (v18, JND; Ex 4.22, 23; Deut 1.31; Hosea 11.1). Following another seven years (as a comparison of the ages of Caleb in Josh 14.7, 10 shows), when Jehovah 'had **destroyed** seven nations in the land of Chanaan, He **divided** their land to them by lot' (v19; Deut 7.1). From the time of Israel's first servitude under Chushanrishathaim (Judg 3.8) to Samuel's anointing of Saul (1 Sam 10.1, 2), God 'gave unto them judges about the space of four hundred and fifty years' (13.20).[17] When they 'desired a king … God **gave** unto them Saul the son of Cis, a man of the tribe of Benjamin, by the space of forty years' (v21). But God removed Saul and, in his place, 'raised up unto them David to be their king; to whom also he gave testimony, and said, I have found David the son of Jesse, a man after Mine own heart, which shall fulfil all My will' (v22; cf. 1 Sam 13.14; Ps 89.20). Paul climaxed his historical résumé by 'leapfrogging' approximately one thousand years to Christ's baptism, when 'God according to His promise **raised** unto Israel a Saviour, Jesus' (vv23-25).

Paul began the soteriological part of his message (vv26-39) with a fresh appeal to his audience: 'Men and brethren, children of the stock of Abraham, and whosoever among you feareth God, to you is the word of this salvation sent' (v26). Because Israel's leaders misunderstood Who Jesus was, despite hearing the clear messianic predictions of their own prophets read every sabbath, they 'fulfilled them in condemning Him' (v27). The nation which had rejected Jehovah and 'desired [*aiteō*] a king' (v21; 1 Sam 8.4-7), also refused the Christ, and 'though they found no cause of death in Him, yet desired [*aiteō*] they Pilate that He should be slain' (v28; Mt 26.59, 60). It was only when every Old Testament prophecy concerning Christ's suffering was accomplished that 'they took Him down from the tree [the cross] and laid Him in a sepulchre' (v29; cf. Deut 21.23).

Within the bounds of divine restraint, men did their worst to Christ, 'but God raised Him from the dead' (v30). Paul used three Old Testament quotations to show that this good news, verified by reliable witnesses (v31; 1 Cor 15.6), had also been promised to Israel's forefathers (vv32, 33). First: 'I will declare the decree: the Lord hath said unto Me, Thou art My Son; this day have I begotten Thee' (Ps 2.7). While the Hebrew word *yālad*, translated 'begotten', 'in its narrowest sense … [describes] the act of a woman in giving birth to a child,'[18] here it refers primarily to God's public declaration of Christ's eternal Sonship when He brought Him forth at the incarnation and presented Him to the nation at His baptism (v33; cf. Mt 3.17). Again, He pronounced His Sonship at the resurrection (Rom 1.4); He will do it once more when Christ rides triumphantly out of heaven to reign (cf. Ps 2.6). Second: 'I will make an everlasting covenant with you, even the sure mercies of David' (Is 55.3). Having outlined Israel's future millennial blessings (Is 54), which will be based on the New Covenant (Jer 31.31), and God's promised mercy to David's seed (2 Sam 7.12-16), Isaiah exhorted thirsty souls to turn to Jehovah for satisfaction (Is 55.1, 2). Since these Davidic mercies can only truly be enjoyed under the unchanging dominion of an ever-living Messiah, Christ's resurrection assured their realisation (v34). Third: 'For thou wilt not leave My soul in hell; neither wilt Thou suffer Thine Holy One to see corruption' (Ps 16.10). In contrast to David's death, burial, and bodily decomposition, while awaiting resurrection, the Saviour's holy body did not decay in the tomb (vv35-37).

Paul appealed to his audience. 'Be it known unto you therefore, men and brethren, that through this man is preached unto you the forgiveness of sins' (v38). Demanding total obedience to all its precepts, and making no provision for presumptuous sins, the Law of Moses was powerless to justify anyone (Ex 19.7, 8; Num 15.30; Gal 3.10-12, 19). In sharp contrast, 'by [Christ] all [including Gentiles] that believe are justified from all things, from which ye could not be justified by the law of Moses' (v39). However, this good news comes with a solemn warning. Using the words of Habakkuk, Paul cautioned his audience that rejection would bring a judgment so severe that they would not even believe the warning of it (vv40, 41; Hab 1.5). Jehovah had previously used the Babylonians to punish His erring people (Hab 1.6-10). In AD 70 God used Roman legions to destroy Jerusalem and disperse the nation. Today, all who reject the gospel will perish eternally in the lake of fire.

'And as they went out they begged that these words might be spoken to them the ensuing sabbath. And the congregation of the synagogue having broken up, many of the Jews and of the worshipping proselytes followed Paul and Barnabas, who speaking to them, persuaded them to continue in the grace of God' (vv42, 43, JND). The confidence they had in Jehovah should now be placed in Christ, His appointed Saviour (cf. Jn 14.1).

When, on the second sabbath, large crowds gathered to hear the missionaries, envious Jews spoke 'against those things which were spoken by Paul, contradicting and blaspheming' (v45). He and Barnabas courageously explained that 'it was necessary that the word of God should first have been spoken to you [the Jews]: but seeing ye put it from you, and judge yourselves unworthy of everlasting life, lo, we turn to the Gentiles' (v46). Because he represented Jehovah's perfect Servant, to Whom it was said, 'I have set Thee to be a light of the Gentiles, that Thou shouldest be for salvation unto the ends of the earth', Paul saw this move as a divine imperative (v47; Is 49.6). His daring announcement delighted the Gentiles, who 'glorified the word of the Lord: and as many as were ordained to eternal life believed' (v48). By word of mouth, 'the word of the Lord was published throughout all the region' (v49). Infuriated, 'the Jews stirred up the devout and honourable women, and the chief men of the city, and raised persecution against Paul and Barnabas, and expelled them out of their coasts' (v50). Far from being downcast, 'they shook off the dust of their feet against them, and came unto Iconium' (v51; Mt 10.14, 15). The missionaries had gone, but the remaining disciples 'were filled with joy, and with the Holy Ghost' (v52).

Iconium, Lystra, and Derbe

Chapter 14 has a 'U-turn' construction. After moving from Iconium to Lystra to Derbe, Paul returned from Derbe to Lystra to

Iconium. Although the geography was the same, the repeat visits had a different purpose. As Paul and Barnabas preached the gospel during the outward journey (vv1, 3, 7, 9, 15-17, 21, 25), they fulfilled the first half of the Great Commission ('preach the gospel to every creature', Mk 16.15). On the return journey, instructing disciples to obey the teachings of the Lord Jesus (vv21-23), they fulfilled the second half of the Great Commission ('teaching them to observe all things whatsoever I have commanded you', Mt 28.19, 20). Even today we should copy this apostolic pattern, preaching the gospel to sinners and teaching the word to saints.

At Iconium, as in Antioch, Paul preached first in the synagogue (v1). This was consistent with God's dispensational dealings (Rom 1.16), as well as a reflection of Paul's burden for his fellow-Israelites (Rom 10.1). The principle for us is that our gospel outreach should start with those who are near to us, who we know well. The primary means for spreading the gospel has always been verbal communication. Since 'faith cometh by hearing and hearing by the word of God' (Rom 10.17), any social enterprise or community engagement should take second place to preaching the word of God. In both public preaching and personal witness, the gospel is meant to be explained using words. Gospel work is essentially straightforward: we sow the seed of God's word; the Lord saves (v1).

Of course, the gospel has always been a polarising message, some accepting it, others rejecting it (v2). Animosity often accompanies rejection. On this occasion the Jews stirred up hostility toward the evangelists. In our day the secular world and its religion, under the subtle influence of 'the god of this world', blinds and poisons the minds of the lost (2 Cor 4.4). Although opposition to the gospel takes many forms, its root is Satan himself. We are at war, 'the weapons of our warfare … [are] not carnal, but mighty through

God to the pulling down of strong holds' (2 Cor 10.4). The spiritual darkness that engulfs the world today should drive us to our knees in prayer.

Although Paul and Barnabas expected opposition, they continued boldly to preach the word. They neither surrendered nor compromised. They did not soften their message or change their approach; they refused to accommodate worldly ideas or means of communication. As faithful stewards of the gospel they continued the work which God had committed to them (1 Cor 4.1, 2). May the Lord help us not to be silenced by the pressure of a secular world, but instead courageously 'preach the word; [and] be instant in season, out of season' (2 Tim 4.2).

Knowing that 'the gospel of Christ … is the power of God unto salvation' (Rom 1.16), Paul and Barnabas laboured on. Arriving at Lystra, they again 'preached the gospel' (v7). Here they encountered a man disabled from birth (v8). Although we cannot comprehend it, Divine sovereignty and human responsibility work hand in hand in salvation, as the healing of this man illustrates. There is a parallel with the blind man whom the Lord healed in the Gospel narrative. God had over-ruled in that man's circumstances (Ex 4.11; Ps 139.13-17), so 'that the works of God should be made manifest in him' (Jn 9.3). The Lord Jesus taught that 'no man can come to Me, except the Father which hath sent Me draw him' (Jn 6.44). On the other hand, Paul appreciated that this man 'had faith to be healed' (v9).

'In writing the book of Acts, Luke seems to have made a special effort to show that everything Peter did, Paul did.'[19] For example, both were visited by an angel, both raised the dead, both were miraculously released from prison, and both healed the lame. In this we see that Paul's credentials equalled Peter's, and the apostle to the Gentiles was not inferior to the apostle of the Jews. It is also a reminder that Jews and Gentiles stand in equal need before God. The gospel abolishes the enmity between Jews and Gentiles, establishing peace between these two warring factions, reconciling both to God in one body. Converted Jews and Gentiles are now viewed as one new man in Christ (Eph 2.15, 16).

The miraculous healing of this lame man confirmed the divine source of the apostles' message (vv10, 11; cf. Mk 16.20). Having said that, although 'the signs of an apostle' (2 Cor 12.12), are not at work today, the salvation of souls and the subsequent change of lives are no less a demonstration of God's power in confirmation of His word.

Although the gospel answers the need of man, sin can create cultural difficulties, as seen when the citizens of Lystra sought to deify Paul and Barnabas (vv11-13). Their ecstatic reaction may partly be explained by the legend that Zeus had once visited a citizen.[20] Paul and Barnabas might have manipulated this situation for their own ends, but refrained, as Paul explains elsewhere: 'we do not, as the many, make a trade of the word of God; but as of sincerity ... before God, we speak in Christ' (2 Cor 2.17, JND). As we make known the gospel, we need to ensure that motives, method, and message are transparent. We must not manipulate people and situations for our own ends. Knowing that people tend to honour men we must point away from ourselves, directing them to the living God.

The apostles humbly confessed that they were 'men with the same nature' (v15, NKJV). Evangelists do not need to be self-deprecating, but rather simply preach repentance towards God and faith in Christ. Paul had no qualms about exposing their idols as 'vanities' (v15), for there is a balance of grace and truth in gospel preaching.

Paul's address to pagans was different from his approach to the Antioch Jews. He adapted his message as the cultural context demanded. Arno C. Gaebelein quotes William Kelly in saying, 'What is notable, I think, especially for all those engaged in the work of the Lord, is the variety in the character of the apostolic addresses. There is no such stiffness as we are apt to find in our day in the preaching of the gospel. Oh, what monotony! What sameness of routine, no matter who may be addressed! We find in the Scripture people dealt with as they were and there is that kind of an appeal to the conscience which was adapted to their peculiar state.'[21]

Although the substance of the gospel never changes, its presentation is open to adaptation. Preaching should not be obscured by jargon or antiquated language. Since western society is increasingly turning away from God, it is wise to emulate Paul's methodology here and on Mars Hill, since the message must be presented in culturally relevant terms.

As to the apostolic preaching continued, so did persecution (v19). Although Paul was especially singled out for ill-treatment (9.16), he reminded the Philippian Christians that 'unto you it is given in the behalf of Christ, not only to believe on Him, but also to suffer for His sake' (Phil 1.29). He later reminded his converts that 'we must through much tribulation enter into the kingdom of God' (14.22). In Iconium Paul escaped harm, but here he was brutally stoned (v19). Sometimes we may escape suffering; at other times God may take us through the eye of the storm. Whatever our circumstances, the Lord can preserve His own (v20).

The unremarkable pivot of the geography of the chapter is full of instruction for the basics of assembly life (v21). Gospel work is often carried out by a few weak believers presenting Christ through the seeming foolishness of preaching. The message is not valued by man, but is highly esteemed by God, we should emulate the consistency and conviction of the apostles.

As Paul and Barnabas retraced their steps homeward, they strengthened the hearts of early converts. Because salvation is not just the memory of past conversion but an ongoing vibrant reality, believers were exhorted 'to continue in the faith' (v22). The Christian life begins and continues with faith. Perseverance is the proof of inner reality. The assemblies in Asia Minor did not need an umbilical cord attached to apostles or organisations. Realising that the work did not depend on them, Paul and Barnabas appointed elders in every assembly, committing them to the Lord (v23). The New Testament shows that assemblies should be autonomous and self-sufficient (not subject to the direction and control of other assemblies or individuals). This, however, does not mean that they are independent of God's word or beyond the spiritual help of other assemblies and individual believers.

May we, with renewed vision and exercise of heart, go out with the gospel and labour in a specific locality, relying on the Lord to save and form companies of His own people. Although the day in which we live is spiritually dark, the Lord has neither changed nor revoked His commission. 'Go labour on, spend and be spent'.

12

JERUSALEM COUNCIL (15.1-35; GAL 2.1-10)

THE DAY OF PENTECOST changed everything. Suddenly, believing Jews and Gentiles were united in Christ, entering equally into the spiritual benefits of the New Covenant, such as regeneration (Jer 32.39, 40; Tit 3.5), the remission of sins (Jer 31.34; 33.8; Eze 36.25; Eph 1.7; 4.32; Col 1.14), and the reception of the Holy Spirit (Isa 59.21; Eze 36.26, 27; 1 Cor 6.19). It was a tremendous jolt to the exclusivist Jewish mindset; and 'there was no small danger lest the new community should be rent asunder almost at its beginning.'[22] How could Jewish Christians associate with believing Gentiles, who did not adhere to the Law of Moses, and whom they had hitherto despised as unclean?

Things came to a head when false Judean teachers, who seem to have claimed the approval of the Jerusalem-based apostles, taught at Antioch, 'except ye be circumcised after the manner of Moses, ye cannot be saved' (v1). As Paul explained later, they were 'false brethren unawares brought in, who came in privily to spy out our liberty which we have in Christ Jesus, that they might bring us into bondage' (Gal 2.4). Having been smuggled in by Satan, they attacked the very foundation of the gospel which offers free salvation through faith in Christ alone. Their demand for Gentile converts to 'be circumcised, and keep the law' troubled the Gentile Christians, 'subverting their souls' (v24). 'Subverting' translates the Greek word *anaskeuazō*, meaning 'an entire removal of goods and chattels either by the owners or by a plundering enemy.'[23] It was a deliberate attempt to rob them of their freshly found Christian joy and liberty, and to split the infant Church.

Concerned that his gospel preaching among the Gentiles would be negated (Gal 2.2), Paul, with Barnabas, had 'no small dissension and disputation with them' (v2). Paul wrote to the Galatians, 'we did not yield in subjection to them for even an hour, so that the truth of the gospel might remain with you' (Gal 2.5, NASB). With Paul receiving divine 'revelation' about the importance of settling the issue (Gal 2.2) and the Antioch church wanting a definitive answer, it was 'determined that Paul and Barnabas, and certain other of them, should go up to Jerusalem unto the apostles and elders about this question' (15.2).

Accompanied by Barnabas and other local Christian brothers, including Titus, Paul travelled to Jerusalem for the third recorded time after his conversion (Gal 2.1). Never wasting a moment, as 'they passed through Phenice and Samaria, [they declared] the conversion of the Gentiles: and they caused great joy unto all the brethren' (v3; cf. Prov 25.25). At Jerusalem, there seems to have been a series of meetings, as follows:

First meeting (Gal 2.1-10)

Realising the seriousness of the situation, Paul wisely arranged a private meeting with the apostles, 'James, Cephas and John', to whom he 'communicated ... that gospel which [he preached] among the Gentiles' (Gal 2.2, 9). While the steadfastness of these apostles had given pillar-like stability to the Jerusalem church, Paul was unfazed by their 'reputation' (Gal 2.2, 6, 9). Nevertheless, he desired their approval. During this discussion, they agreed that the Gentile Titus did not require circumcision (Gal 2.1, 3) and added nothing to the gospel Paul preached (Gal 2.6). Rather, recognising the same power of God which 'wrought effectually in Peter to the apostleship of the circumcision ... was mighty in [Paul] toward the Gentiles' and perceiving 'the grace that was given unto [Paul], they gave to [Paul] and Barnabas the right hands of fellowship; that [Paul and Barnabas] *should go* unto the heathen, and they unto the circumcision' (Gal 2.7-9). Their only proviso was 'that [Paul and Barnabas] should remember the poor' (Gal 2.10).

Second meeting (15.4, 5)

Having secured the private support of the apostles, Paul and his companions reported to the whole Jerusalem church 'all things that God had done with them' (v4). Pharisee converts insisted 'it was needful to circumcise [Gentile believers], and to command *them* to keep the law of Moses' (v5). This prompted a third meeting.

Third meeting (15.6-21)

The apostles and elders then 'came together for to consider of this matter' (v6). After 'much disputing', Peter reminded them that God had chosen him to evangelize Cornelius and his Gentile friends (v7; Acts 10, 11). When these Gentiles believed, 'God, which knoweth the hearts, bare them **witness**, giving them the Holy Ghost, even as *he did* unto [the Jewish believers]' (v8). Any attempt to burden Gentile converts with the unbearable yoke of God's law, which the Jews never managed to keep, was putting 'God to the test' (v10, NASB). Peter concluded that neither Jews nor Gentiles are saved by law keeping but 'through the grace of the Lord Jesus Christ' (v11). Peter's last recorded words in the Acts of the Apostles were so persuasive that 'all the multitude kept silence, and gave audience to Barnabas and Paul, declaring what miracles and **wonders** God had wrought among the Gentiles by them' (v12).

James directed them to God's **word** (vv13-21). In the Old Testament, Jehovah visited Israel and dwelt among them as a special people linked to His name (Ex 4.31; 25.8; Deut 7.6; 12.5; 14.21; Jer 13.11). The early conversion of Cornelius was a similar visitation by God, this time to Gentiles, 'to take out of them a people for his name' (v14). This correlated well with the Jewish scriptures: 'to this agree the words of the prophets' (v15; Amos 9.11-15). Amos foresaw David's dynasty restored to its former glory, Israel vanquishing her foes and established prosperously in her land (Amos 9.11-15). By replacing Amos' phrase 'in that day' with 'I will return' (Amos 9.11; Acts 15.16; cf. Jer 12.15), James indicated that this prophecy will be fulfilled completely at Messiah's coming. The Septuagint translators altered the phrase 'that they may possess the remnant of Edom' (Amos 9.12) to read 'that the residue of men might seek after the Lord' (10.17). The Hebrew text emphasised Israel's victory over her enemies. The Greek translation showed that Gentile nations will seek Jehovah. Both doctrines are true. The Hebrew and Greek texts agreed that the heathen will be 'called by [Jehovah's] name' (Amos 9.12; Acts 15.17), exactly what James had said of Cornelius and his friends. Gentile conversions within the church era do not exhaust Amos' prediction but are entirely consistent with the eternal plan of God, Who has 'known ... all his works from the beginning of the world' (v18).

James therefore counselled that 'we trouble not them, which from among the Gentiles are turned to God: but that we write unto them, that they abstain from pollutions of idols, and *from* fornication, and *from* things strangled, and *from* blood' (vv19, 20). True unity requires a careful balance of give and take without compromising truth (cf. Rom 14.3). Jewish believers would not impose Law keeping and circumcision on Gentiles; neither should Gentile Christians engage in anything associated with idolatry which would be odious to their Jewish brethren. The 'pollutions of idols' referred to the 'meats offered to idols' (vv20, 29). Since these animals were often strangled to death their corpses retained the blood which Jews were forbidden from eating (Lev 17.10, 11).

In the immediate context, the 'fornication' mentioned was probably those sexual relations with closely related family members which Moses proscribed (cf. Lev 18.6-18). James finished by assuring his Jewish hearers that the Law would never be forgotten. If any Gentile wanted to learn more about it, 'Moses of old time hath in every city them that preach him, being read in the synagogues every sabbath day' (v21).

Fourth meeting (15.22-29)

Under the Spirit's direction, 'the whole church' at Jerusalem agreed to write to their Gentile brethren at Antioch. The letter was brief, courteous, and authoritative. After a warm greeting, they firmly disassociated themselves from the false teachers, commanded the Antioch believers to abstain from everything associated with idolatry, and wished them well (vv23-29).

Conclusion (15.30-35)

For verbal confirmation, Paul and Barnabas were accompanied by two of Jerusalem's own highly respected men: Judas and Silas (vv22, 23, 25-28). As soon as the Antioch believers read the letter, 'they rejoiced for the consolation' (vv30, 31). Judas and Silas then exhorted and confirmed the brethren, and 'tarried there a space' before returning to Jerusalem (vv32, 33). Afterwards, Silas seems to have returned to Antioch and joined Paul and Barnabas, 'teaching and preaching the word of the Lord, with many others also' (vv34, 35).

13

PAUL'S SECOND MISSIONARY JOURNEY
(15.36-18.22)

SHARING THE GOSPEL with those around us is one of the most valuable yet difficult activities in which we can engage. It is valuable because it meets man's greatest need and is at the same time a practical demonstration of our confidence in the atonement. It is difficult since we know it may well provoke a hostile reception, and, like Jeremiah, we may feel terrified (Jer 1.17). With that in mind, before tracing Paul's second missionary journey, let us see what we can learn from Paul to help us in our own evangelism. What made him an effective gospel preacher?

A commitment to care for his converts

Paul's second missionary journey began as a follow up visit to believers converted on a past mission: 'Let us go again and visit our brethren in every city where we have preached the word of the Lord and see how they do' (15.36). Just as a parent's interest in a child does not end at his or her birth, Paul wanted to see spiritual growth in those who believed. Post-conversion progress is God's explicit will for believers (1 Tim 2.4). To this end, Paul taught new Christians about baptism (Lydia 16.15, Jailor 16.33, Crispus & other Corinthians 18.8), gave them initial spiritual instruction (16.32; 18.11), and enjoyed fellowship with them (Lydia's house 16.15, 40; the Jailor's house 16.34). He saw to it that believers were 'established in the faith' (16.5). Far from being an afterthought, Paul's concern for the spiritual well-being of believers, young and old, was a priority. We too ought to share this ambition.

Carefully chosen co-workers

The surprising fall-out between Paul and Barnabas warns us that Christian service may be complex – friction comes not only from the world but also from fellow believers, with whom we do not see eye to eye. The question that divided them was whether Mark, who returned home midway through the last journey (13.13), should come on this one. Paul evidently felt that a difficult missionary journey was not the place for Mark to prove himself. When Mark later showed his usefulness again Paul was willing to recognise this (2 Tim 4.11), indicating that Paul was not here writing him off permanently. But on this occasion Paul chose those whose most recent track record indicated they would undoubtedly bolster the trip. Silas had a joyful confidence in the Lord, even under stress, a confidence displayed when he sang and prayed with Paul in prison (16.2; cf. James 5.13). Timothy was selected for his good reputation (16.2), for there is little more harmful to the gospel than servants whose bad behaviour attracts criticism. Let us aim to be exemplary co-workers and choose our fellow workers wisely.

Good Habits

When Paul entered a new city, he had a well-practised routine: he went first to the synagogue to speak with the Jews (17.2, 10, 17, 18.4), and then to the marketplace to speak with the Gentiles (17.17). This order reflected the Jews' priority in privilege and responsibility (1.8; Rom 1.16). Even more fundamentally, this strategy allowed Paul to engage with people – an essential ingredient in evangelism. In the synagogue he addressed a semi-interested audience. In the marketplace he created an interest by one-to-one conversations which, in turn, led to the larger opportunity on Mars Hill. Paul favoured opportunities that provided prolonged exposure to his audience – he spent three weeks in Thessalonica (17.2); at Corinth he preached weekly for 18 months, and then stayed on for 'a good while' (18.4, 11, 18). Those with whom we have prolonged contact (e.g., family, friends, neighbours, colleagues) are often the hardest to evangelise, but with the Lord's help we can find opportunities to speak one-to–one, just as Paul did in Athens.

Perseverance in the face of many difficulties

Paul faced formidable problems during his second journey. These included the following: in-house dissention with Barnabas (15.39); divinely arranged disruption in travel plans (16.16, 7); satanically generated, undesirable publicity (16.16-18); commercial opposition leading to unjust punishment and imprisonment (16.9, 37); religious hostility (17.5, 13; 18.6), and the continuing threat of further violence about which Paul received special reassurance from the Lord (18.9, 10). Given such challenges, it is understandable that Paul vetoed Mark's presence on the journey. He seems to have expected a tough time (9.16). But none of these difficulties deterred Paul; they simply brought out his perseverance. His purpose being to preach the gospel, he remained undaunted by the attendant dangers (21.13). May the Lord grant us similar perseverance.

Faithfulness to the Scriptures

Paul preached a message his hearers could verify by comparing Paul's word with God's. This is clearly demonstrated in the case of the Bereans, who 'received the word…searched the scriptures whether those things were so…therefore many of them believed' (17.11, 12). Because of this link between actively searching the scriptures and experiencing saving faith, preachers must base their message on the word of God, which alone produces genuine faith (Rom 10.17; 1 Cor 2.4, 5). This has several ramifications. Do I quote the Bible when explaining the gospel? Do I remember that it is God's truth, not the cleverness of my presentation, that has power to save? Does the way I explain the gospel bear up to scrutiny against the word of God? If I simply 'preach the word', it will.

Adaptability to his audience

Paul pitched his message to the understanding of his audience. To those with a background in the Old Testament he reasoned 'from the scriptures' that 'Christ must needs have suffered and risen again from the dead;' and 'that this Jesus, whom I preach unto you, is Christ' (17.2, 3, 11; 18.5). By contrast, at Mars Hill, when preaching to Gentile philosophers, he appealed not directly to the scriptures, of which they were ignorant, but to their conscience. His assertions, however, were in perfect harmony with the word, as he began with God as the Creator and Sustainer of all, went on to expose the inadequacy of his audience's view of God, as witnessed by their idols, and finally called them to repentance in light of a coming time of reckoning (17.30). This flow of thought parallels his argument for man's guilt based on our inner consciousness of sin in Romans chapters 1 and 2. As well as using material suited to his audience, Paul communicated in a logical manner. He 'spoke' (16.3), 'reasoned' (17.2, 17; 18.4), 'opened and alleged' (17.3), and 'preached' (17.13). The gospel can be shared in a variety of contexts ranging from every-day conversation and interactive discussion to direct proclamation and appeal.

A passion for the lost

Paul did not preach the gospel reluctantly; he was compelled from deep within his soul. On at least two occasions, Luke notes his passion to preach. In Athens, 'his spirit was stirred in him when he saw the city wholly given to idolatry' (17.16). In Corinth, he was 'pressed in the spirit and testified to the Jews that Jesus was the

Christ' (18.5). Knowing God's truth had set him free and seeing the needs of others, he could not be silent. As God opens our eyes to the blinding and binding reality of sin we too will be impelled to speak. Paul's love for the lost fostered real courage – he was alone in Athens when on Mars Hill he boldly confronted the idolatry of his audience. While valuing the help of co-labourers, he knew his sufficiency came ultimately from the Lord (18.10; 2 Cor 3.5, 6; 2 Tim 4.16, 17).

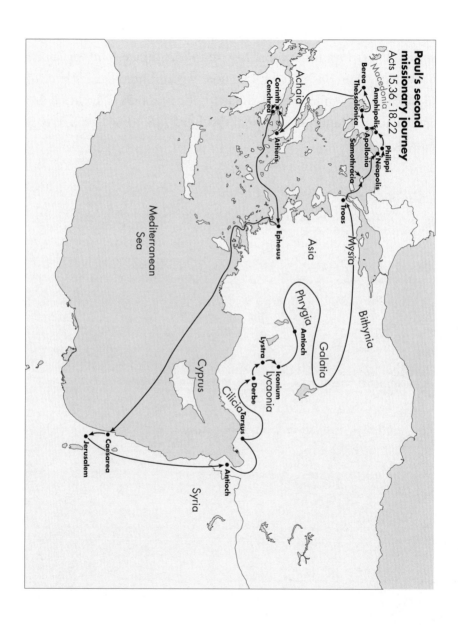

14

PREACHING AT PHILIPPI (16.6-40)

THE MISSIONARIES' ARRIVAL AT PHILIPPI – the first major city of that part of Macedonia – marked a significant movement of the gospel westwards into Europe (v12). Philippi was located on a plain between the Pangaeus and Haemus mountain ranges, approximately nine miles from the Mediterranean. Being on the Egnatian Way, an important Roman highway spanning Macedonia from east to west, Philippi was an accessible city. It had local gold mines, exceptionally fertile soil, and a medical school, but no synagogue. While Paul's habit was to begin preaching at the local synagogue, at Philippi he started 'by a river side, where prayer was wont to be made' (v13). As a Roman 'colony' (v12), Philippi enjoyed all the privileges of Roman citizenship (including exemption from taxation and flogging), a status which was highly valued by its population (vv20, 21).

Giants of human history had cast their shadow on the city. It was originally founded in BC 350 by Philip of Macedon, the father of Alexander the Great. Octavian, the adopted son of Julius Caesar and the future Caesar Augustus, in partnership with Mark Antony, vanquished Marcus Brutus and Cassius at the battle of Philippi in BC 42. Seeing the inevitability of defeat, Brutus fell on his sword. After the battle, veteran soldiers were released to colonise the city.

The missionaries

Approximately 100 years after the battle of Philippi the Apostle Paul, with Luke, Silas, and Timothy, evangelised the city. Although a diverse group, these four men were united in their desire to spread the gospel. Luke, the author of Acts, was a Gentile doctor who marked his joining the missionary party at Troas with a simple narrative shift from 'they' to 'we' (16.8-10). He remained at Philippi while the others passed on to Amphipolis (17.1), perhaps spending time at the medical school. Under the inspiration of the Holy Spirit, Paul and Luke wrote more than half the New Testament. Silas, the third member of the missionary band, had been a well-respected Christian at the Jerusalem church (15.12).

Timothy was the youngest member of the team. His devotion to the Lord is evident throughout the New Testament. Paul viewed him as his own spiritual son (1 Tim 1.2; 2 Tim 1.2; 2.1). It is likely that he had witnessed first-hand God's power at work in Paul's life (14.8-10), his humility (14.11-18) and his steadfastness in the face of severe opposition (14.19-21; 2 Tim 3.10, 11), as well as his genuine concern for the spiritual well-being of new converts (14.21-23). Whether or not Timothy was converted under Paul's preaching at Lystra during the first missionary journey, it is clear that a solid foundation of Bible knowledge had been laid up in his heart from childhood, probably by his believing grandmother and mother (2 Tim 1.5; 3.15). Being 'well reported of by the brethren' in two local churches, Timothy was active in the Lord's service before becoming a missionary (v2). Despite the discomfort involved, the half-Jewish, half-Gentile Timothy submitted to Paul's advice and was circumcised, thus avoiding any needless offence to local Jews (v3; cf. 1 Cor 9.20).

The Holy Spirit led the missionaries westward (vv6, 7, 9), prevented them from going south 'to preach the word in Asia' (v6), and stopped them moving north into Bithynia (v7). Through a night vision to Paul the missionaries were called westward into Macedonia (v9). They promptly obeyed the divine call, endeavouring 'to go into Macedonia, assuredly gathering that the Lord had called [them] for to preach the gospel unto them' (v10). While believers today do not rely on visions for divine guidance, as the sons of God they are still led by the Holy Spirit (Rom 8.14). Much of this leading takes the form of illumination from God's word and the application of its principles. Of course, such obedience to the word proves love for Christ (Jn 14.15).

Although this world's culture is obsessed with the visual, we must follow the apostolic example and preach 'the word' (v6), communicating with verbal clarity the gospel message. Although the missionaries began by speaking to a small group of religious women (v13), news spread quickly about these 'servants of the Most High God, which shew ... the way of salvation' (v17). Since this good news comes from God (Rom 1.1), and men are naturally opposed to God (Rom 5.10), not only is suffering an inevitable part of the Christian life (14.22; Phil 1.28-30; 2 Tim 3.13), but any clear presentation of the gospel inevitably arouses hostility. This opposition began with a demon-possessed girl who, while acknowledging the true character and message of the missionaries, attempted to hamper their service. Nothing of lasting value can be achieved for the Lord without prayer (v16). Paul expelled the demon, but the text does not state whether the girl was converted (v18). Since she and her soothsaying abilities had enriched her owners (v16), the exorcism and subsequent loss of revenue prompted a violent response. Paul and Silas were apprehended, stripped, beaten with rods and 'thrust ... into the inner prison' (vv22-24). But they were not downcast. They did not complain that God's guidance led to suffering. Instead, 'at midnight Paul and Silas prayed, and sang praises unto God' (v25), their witness resulting in the jailor's conversion. In difficult circumstances it is right to be 'careful for nothing; but in everything by prayer and supplication with thanksgiving let [our] requests be made known unto God' (Phil 4.6). Believers should remain joyful, knowing that 'the joy of the Lord is your strength' (Neh 8.10). Since the ungodly watch us, God may also speak to sinners through our reaction to adversity.

The converts

Lydia and the jailor were different individuals with different conversions. Lydia was a wealthy businesswoman who traded in 'purple' (v14), an expensive dye which was extracted from the neck glands of Mediterranean shellfish. Being religiously inclined, Lydia listened attentively to the words of the missionaries (vv13, 14). The Lord quietly opened her heart so that 'she attended unto the things which were spoken of Paul' (v14).

The jailor, on the other hand, appeared indifferent to the gospel and callous in his management of the freshly beaten missionaries, thrusting 'them into the inner prison, and [making] their feet fast in the stocks' (v24). It took a finely tuned earthquake (which shook the prison's foundations, opened its doors, and loosed its prisoners' bands, v26) to bring him to an end of himself. Assuming his prisoners had escaped and knowing the severe punishment for such failure, 'he drew out his sword, and would have killed himself' (v27). But his life was preserved by Paul crying out, 'Do thyself no harm: for we are all here' (v28); and in the middle of the night 'he called for a light, and sprang in, and came trembling, and fell down before Paul and Silas, and brought them out, and said, Sirs, what must I do to be saved?' (vv29, 30). Of course, the answer to this urgent, personal question was not to 'do' anything but rather 'believe' (v32).

As soon as they believed the gospel, Lydia, the jailor, and his household were all baptized (vv15, 33), symbolising their association with Christ's death, burial, and resurrection, as well as an internal transformation in their lives (Rom 6.1-5). Their subsequent behaviour verified this change. Lydia eagerly showed hospitality to the missionaries (v15). The jailor, who had treated them harshly, now 'washed their stripes ... [and] set meat before them' (vv33, 34). Relieved of his terror (v29), 'he rejoiced, believing in God with all his house' (v34). Truly, 'if any man be in Christ, he is a new creature: old things are passed away; behold, all things are become new' (2 Cor 5.17).

Paul's relationship with the church at Philippi continued through the years. Ten years later, while imprisoned in Rome (28.16-31), Paul received a gift from the Philippian Christians. He wrote a letter to thank them (Phil 4.10-20), confirming his affection for them (Phil 1.8; 4.1). He still prayed for them (Phil 1.9) and with the skill of a true shepherd, ever watchful for God's people, he encouraged them to live godly lives (Phil 1.27). He warned against the danger of Judaizing teachers (Phil 3.2) and exhorted them to be united (Phil 1.27; 2.2; 4.2). As well as reminding them of his own example, he urged them to follow the pattern of other godly Christians (Phil 3.17), all the time foregrounding the Lord Jesus as their ultimate model (Phil 2.5-8).

15

THESSALONICA, BEREA, AND ATHENS (17.1-31)

IN THIS CHAPTER PAUL covers about 300 miles, beginning in Thessalonica, stopping off at Berea, and ending in Athens. His movements are prompted by a troublesome group of Jews who, resentful of the gospel, hounded him from city to city. However, their opposition did not stop Paul preaching, it simply moved his platform. Acts 17 demonstrates that there will always be a reaction when the gospel is preached, ranging from the outright fury of these Thessalonian Jews to the noble faith of the Bereans. Paul's address on Mars Hill in Athens provides a template of how to preach the gospel to an audience with no Bible background.

Far from welcoming Paul's scriptural argument that Jesus was the long-promised Messiah, a vocal group of Jews in the Thessalonian Synagogue reacted with envy-fuelled fury, hiring local thugs to stir up a riot. They failed to hurt Paul but Jason, his host, was caught in the crossfire. The angry reaction prompted Paul's departure to Berea, leaving the new Thessalonian converts in a hostile environment (1 Thess 2.14-16), although firmly sustained by Paul's prayers (1 Thess 3.10). Not content with driving Paul out of Thessalonica, the Jews followed him to Berea where they repeated their disturbances, again prompting Paul to move on. What are we to learn? The evangelist is under no obligation to stay around to endure unhelpful confrontation. In fact, outright rejection seems to be one of the means the Lord uses to move His messengers to a new audience. Paul repeatedly faced opposition and repeatedly moved on (v10, v14, v33; cf. Lk 9.5; Acts 13.46). Ironically, adversity serves to spread the word!

When Paul preached Christ from the Old Testament in the Thessalonian synagogue 'some of them believed', but in the Berean synagogue the response was better, not just because 'many believed', but because of how they came to belief. They listened open-mindedly to Paul, checked what he said against the scriptures, and then trusted the Lord. Their rigour earned the commendation of 'noble', and provides some striking lessons for preachers and listeners today:

Lesson 1. If the Bereans are commended for cross-checking the teaching of the great apostle against the scriptures, how much more should we assess preachers today in the light of the word of God? It is all too easy to sit under the preached word without having our critical faculties properly engaged, let alone imitating the follow up investigation at home which the Bereans practised.

Lesson 2. If Paul preached in a way that allowed his hearers to check the message against his source and come to the same conclusions, then he must have allowed the scriptures to speak for themselves. There is nothing to beat contextual exposition of the Bible.

Lesson 3. Faith is not a leap in the dark. The Bereans show that it involves intelligent surrender to the truth of the word. Paul's preaching demonstrated that Christ accurately fulfilled Old Testament prophecies, proving that the gospel is not from men but from God.

While waiting in Athens for his travelling companions, Paul saw an idolatry epidemic which provoked an irresistible urge to proclaim God's truth. He began with conversations in the synagogue and marketplace, but was soon invited to address a group of philosophers from the Areopagus. It is encouraging to note that it was Paul's faithfulness in one-to-one evangelism that created the opportunity. His presentation of the gospel is a model in how to approach those with no background in the scriptures. The climax of his message is summed up in verse 30: 'God now commandeth all men everywhere to repent'.

Among Athens' many shrines Paul found an altar inscribed 'To the unknown god', an apt starting point. As the local people were evidently confused about God, it was necessary to clearly make Him known. Paul did this by boldly proclaiming God as the singular, supreme, creating, sustaining and sovereign director of the Universe. This flew in the face of their idolatry and cut across their impoverished concept of deity: the one true God does not need a man-made building to live in, nor does he need offerings. In fact, the reverse is true. Humans are dependent on Him for everything, for God 'giveth to all life, and breath and all things'. Thus, Paul was presenting the gospel as the **ultimate** message because of the unique greatness of the God from whom it comes.

While the Athenians occupied their day discussing, debating, and endlessly looking for new ideas, Paul presented the gospel as an **urgent** message from the God who 'now commandeth'. The gospel is not an idea to be admired, a theory to be debated, or a lifestyle to be chosen. It is a command from the Lord of the Universe to be obeyed. It presents mankind as being in rebellion against God yet provides an opportunity for rebellion to be replaced with obedience. If obeyed, the gospel brings eternal blessing, if ignored it seals one's eternal doom (1 Pet 4.17). The urgency of the gospel stems from the fact that an eternal destiny rests on a temporal choice. The preacher must insist that 'now is the day of salvation' (2 Cor 6.2), because one of the evils of the human heart is to presume on God's longsuffering (Rom 2.4, 5) and delay in responding to His mercy.

The call of the gospel goes out to 'all men everywhere' showing it is a **universal** message. The word used for 'men' is *anthropos*, indicating a human being, male or female. Gender, age, nationality, and country of residence are immaterial. Further, no chosen worldview can exempt us from the gospel's summons. Atheist or agnostic, religious or irreligious – God recognises no man-made exemption certificate. There is not a more universal, relevant message.

The gospel is an **uncomfortable** message because at its centre is a call 'to repent.' Repentance involves a change of mind, a turning from whatever mistaken belief we may have, to a belief in the truth of God. For the atheist it involves an admission that he has been a fool (Ps 14.1; 19.1). For the agnostic there is the admission that he has suppressed his consciousness of God's existence (Rom 1.19, 20). For the do-gooder there must be the admission that his good works are like filthy rags before God (Is 64.6, Eph 2.8-10), while anyone who thinks there are many ways to God must repent and come to Him via the one Mediator, Jesus Christ (1 Tim 2.5). The gospel is hard to stomach because it involves a contrite confession of wrongness and neediness, but when the sinner is in that state, he is precisely in the place where God's grace reaches him (Is 66.2).

Lastly, the gospel is an **unavoidable** message, 'because he hath appointed a day, in the which He will judge the world in righteousness by that man whom he hath ordained; whereof he hath given assurance to all men in that he hath raised him from the dead.' The resurrection of the Lord Jesus is God's pledge to all that death is not the end. There is a Day of Judgment ahead, and each one of us will stand before God's chosen Judge (Rom 2.6). All who have ever lived will be resurrected (Jn 5.28.29) in what will be a stunning display of divine power. Christ's resurrection is the guarantee that all will be raised. Those who have obeyed the gospel can face this day with confidence (1 Jn 4.17), being safe in Christ with a righteousness equal to that of the Righteous Judge Himself (Phil 3.9; 2 Tim 4.8). However, those who have disobeyed the gospel will face the terrible reality of God awakening in judgment on them (Ps 73.20). Reflecting on this truth should sort out our priorities and motivate us to witness.

Finally, just as the message Paul announced in Athens exemplifies what we must preach, so the reactions of his hearers are typical of what we might expect. Firstly, some mocked (v32a), because the human heart unaided by Spirit of God thinks the things of God are foolish (1 Cor 2.14). Others procrastinated (v32b), perhaps sensing something of the weight of the message yet not wanting their comfort disturbed. This was to presume on the longsuffering of God. But the abundance of God's grace was displayed in the fact that some believed (v34). Thus, the divine purpose was accomplished: 'Great is the mystery of godliness: God was...preached unto the Gentiles, believed on in the world' (1 Tim 3.16).

16

CONVERSIONS AT CORINTH (18.1-22)

Corinth was the chief city of the Roman senatorial province (belonging to the senate) of Achaia. In contrast to Roman imperial provinces (belonging to the emperor), there was no military presence. The city was 'dominated by the Acrocorinth (566 metres), a steep, flat topped rock surmounted by the acropolis, which in ancient times contained, *inter alia*, a temple of Aphrodite, goddess of love'[24] served by more than 1,000 religious prostitutes. Set on an isthmus between the Ionian and Aegean seas, Corinth was labelled 'the city of the two seas.' Having three harbours – Cenchrea eastward (v18), Lechaeum westward, and Schoenus where the isthmus was narrowest – Corinth developed into a successful trading centre, its local manufacture of porcelain and ceramics adding to its wealth. The population of about 100,000 was constantly changing, the relatively short stay of Aquila and Priscilla not being unusual (18.2, 18). This rapid turnover of inhabitants, coupled with the political stability of the Roman Empire, made Corinth an ideal place for evangelism, since the message could spread rapidly throughout the region.

The unusually high concentration of Jews in Corinth at that time, due to Emperor Claudius' recent expulsion of them from Rome, swelled Paul's immediate synagogue audience (vv2, 4). It also exposed an underlying Gentile anti-Semitism, which has showed itself in the harsh treatment of Jewish people throughout the centuries. En route through Europe to the Holy Land, 'the barbarous crusaders ... offered Jews baptism or death.'[25] In AD

1290, having confiscated Jewish assets, Edward I ousted all Jews from Britain.[26] Sadly, even professing Christians have entertained this anti-Semitic worldview. In his last ever public sermon, Martin Luther, the great reformer, 'pleaded that all Jews should be expelled from Germany.'[27]

Gallio was Corinth's proconsul (v12). He had been adopted into the family of Julius Gallio, a famous rhetorician. Because of his affable disposition, he was nicknamed 'Dulcis [sweet] Gallio.' While diligent in his work, he was wise enough not to get involved in petty Jewish squabbles, in this case their religious accusations against Paul (vv14-17). This discretion preserved the apostle from a further beating as well as giving local Gentiles an opportunity to vent their anti-Semitic tendency by beating Sosthenes, the chief ruler of the synagogue (v17). Interestingly, it seems that Sosthenes was subsequently converted (1 Cor 1.1).

The preacher

Paul lived a turbulent life, marked by relentless change and challenges (2 Cor 11.23-28). In this case he travelled from Athens to Corinth, moving 'from a quiet provincial town to the busy metropolis of a province, and from the seclusion of an ancient university to the seat of government and trade.'[28] Nonetheless, in every situation he was content (Phil 4.11, 12), always toiling beyond the call of duty. At Thessalonica he had laboured 'night and day, because [he] would not be chargeable unto any of [them]' (1 Thess 2.9). Similarly, at Corinth he waived the rights of apostles and gospel preachers to be financially funded (1 Cor 9.1-18; 2 Cor 11.7-9), working as a tent maker to support himself. By doing this Paul eliminated any implication that he served for financial gain (1 Thess 2.5), he provided practical example of the importance of work (1 Thess 4.11, 12), and he avoided overburdening the Corinthian believers (2 Cor 12.13).

Having a deep longing for the Jewish people (Rom 9.1-5; 10.1), as was his pattern, Paul began preaching in the synagogue (v4). And this he did with unshakeable conviction. 'Reasoned' (v4) translates the Greek word *dialegomai*, meaning 'to ponder, then to dispute with others.'[29] Paul's strong belief in his message was bolstered by years of intensive Bible study, because it is a 'firm grasp of the word of God and an ever-growing absorption of its truthfulness into the fabric of one's life [which] are the underpinning upon which convictions rest.'[30] He steadfastly preached 'every Sabbath' (v4; cf. 1 Cor 15.58), his fervour increasing with the arrival of Silas and Timothy. Being 'pressed in the Spirit, [he] testified to the Jews that Jesus [of Nazareth, Who they had rejected] was Christ [God's anointed]' (v5). Despite his immense intellect and comprehensive education, Paul kept his message simple, preaching 'Jesus Christ, and Him crucified' (1 Cor 2.1, 2).

Paul faced fierce Jewish opposition – 'opposed' translates the Greek word *antitasso*, meaning to make war against. He reacted by turning away from them: 'he shook his raiment, and said unto them, your blood be upon your own heads; I am clean: from henceforth I will go unto the Gentiles' (v6; cf. Eze 3.18; 18.13; 33.4-8). Howbeit, his yearning for his Jewish brethren meant that he did not go far – only to a 'house joined hard to the synagogue' (v6) – still giving them opportunity to repent. What was the result? 'Crispus, the chief ruler of the synagogue, believed on the Lord with all his house; and many of the Corinthians hearing believed, and were baptized' (v8).

As seen at Corinth, church planting takes a long time. It needs the Lord's power and protection and should follow the instructions of the great commission: 'And Jesus came and spake unto them, saying, All power is given unto me in heaven and in earth. Go ye therefore, and teach all nations, baptizing them in the name of the Father, and of the Son, and of the Holy Ghost: teaching them to observe all things whatsoever I have commanded you: and, lo, I am with you alway, *even* unto the end of the world. Amen' (Mt 28.18-20). At Corinth God showed His power to touch any life by saving the chief ruler of the synagogue. Those who believed the gospel message were baptized (v8). The Lord allayed Paul's fears with the words: 'Be not afraid, but speak, and hold not thy peace: For I am with thee, and no man shall set on thee to hurt thee: for I have much people in this city. And he continued *there* a year and six months, teaching the word of God among them.' (18.9-11). Such a protracted period of Bible teaching ensured that the newly formed church was well established in the truth of God.

The people

The church at Corinth has been described in various ways, each depicting different aspects of its character. As 'the church [*ekklēsia*] of God which is at Corinth', it is a called-out company of people, separated to the God of heaven, 'sanctified in Christ Jesus, called *to be* saints' (1 Cor 1.2). As 'God's husbandry [*giōrgion*, a farm]' (1 Cor 3.9), the assembly is likened to a field in which God worked, with fruitfulness being the goal. The figures of a 'building' or 'temple' remind us that God, by His Holy Spirit, indwells each local church (1 Cor 3.9, 16, 17). The metaphor of the body implies unity amongst the members despite their diverse functions (1 Cor 12.27). As a 'chaste virgin' the church at Corinth was expected to be holy (2 Cor 11.2). As 'the epistle of Christ' the assembly was a message read by others (2 Cor 3.3), for unbelievers carefully marked the behaviour of local saints, as they do today.

As it developed, the assembly had many positive features. It was 'enriched … in all utterance, and in all knowledge' (1 Cor 1.5), spiritually gifted and consciously awaiting Christ's return (1 Cor 1.7). Having been bought with a price (1 Cor 6.20), the Christians' lives had been transformed at conversion (1 Cor 6.9-11). They were zealous of spiritual gifts (1 Cor 14.12), keen both to support poor saints (1 Cor 16.1, 2; 2 Cor 9.1, 2) and to pray for the apostle Paul (2 Cor 1.11).

Sadly, the church at Corinth also displayed severe deficiencies. It became divided (1 Cor 1.11; 11.18, 19), with saints going to law against each other (1 Cor 6.1) and using their spiritual liberty carelessly (1 Cor 8.9-13; 10.24). Full of envy (1 Cor 3.1-3) and pride (1 Cor 4.6, 7, 8, 10, 18), the assembly remained spiritually immature, unable to cope with advanced Christian doctrine (1 Cor 3.1-3). Fornication (1 Cor 5.1), idolatry (1 Cor 10.14), ungodliness (2 Cor 12.21; 13.2), and even a denial of the resurrection (1 Cor 15.12) infiltrated its ranks. Some members were audacious enough to challenge Paul's apostleship and godly character (1 Cor 9.1-3; 2 Cor 10.2). Denying headship (1 Cor 11.13-16) and exhibiting selfishness in love feasts, which were directly linked to the Lord's Supper, eventually led to disciplinary illness and ultimately to death (1 Cor 11.20-22, 30). Because such failures can appear quickly in a local church it is vital for all believers, especially elders, to remain constantly vigilant.

Homeward bound (vv18-22)

Accompanied by Aquila and Priscilla, Paul sailed from Corinth to Ephesus and onwards to Caesarea. Having gone up to Jerusalem 'and saluted the church', Paul returned to Antioch, where he undoubtedly gathered the believers and rehearsed all that God had done during this second missionary journey.

17

PAUL'S THIRD MISSIONARY JOURNEY (18.23-21.17)

THROUGHOUT HIS THIRD missionary journey, Paul showed a genuine concern for God's people and an unyielding determination to do the right thing. He performed miracles, worked to support himself, and, despite intense opposition, would not compromise the gospel.

Paul had a true shepherd's heart. After planting local churches, he revisited them and wrote to them. 'Having spent some time [in Antioch], he departed and passed successively through the Galatian region and Phrygia, strengthening all the disciples' (18.23, NASB). Arriving at Ephesus, he discovered about twelve disciples who had neither received the Holy Spirit nor been 'baptized in the name of the Lord Jesus' (20.1-7). Having corrected their misunderstanding, he went on to preach in the synagogue for four months (19.8). When resisted, he disputed daily for two years in Tyrannus' school, 'so that all they which dwelt in Asia heard the word of the Lord Jesus …' (20.9, 10). A public outcry ended his time at Ephesus (19.23-41).

Paul sailed to Macedonia to teach and encourage the believers (20.1, 2). Three months in Greece ended with a Jewish assassination plot, necessitating a return through Macedonia to Philippi, where Luke re-joined him, and from where he sailed to Troas (20.3-6). There Paul broke bread with the believers, taught them late into the night, and restored a young man to life (20.7-12).

Wishing time alone, Paul walked from Troas to Assos while his companions took ship (20.13). The missionary group then sailed down the western coast of Asia Minor to Miletus, where Paul met and exhorted the Ephesian elders (20.14-28). After this, they sailed to Tyre and spent seven days with local believers (21.1-6). Sailing onward to Ptolemais, they met with the Christians for one day (21.7). On reaching Caesarea, they stayed with Philip the evangelist (21.7-9). Despite repeated warnings, Paul went on to Jerusalem, where he was soon imprisoned. This imprisonment lasted to the end of the Acts of the Apostles.

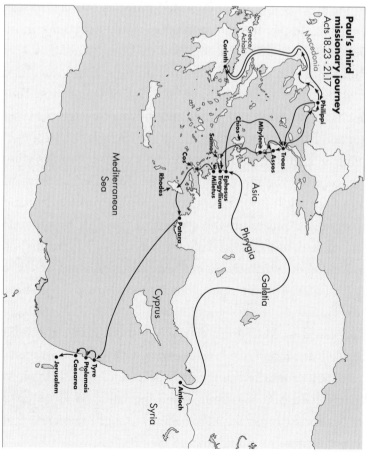

18

EVANGELISING EPHESUS (18.24-20.1)

FOUNDED BY ALEXANDER THE GREAT in BC 332, Alexandria grew rapidly into the world's biggest city, holding the largest urban Jewish community anywhere, and becoming a respected centre of Greek culture and learning. It was here, sometime between BC 250-150, that the Septuagint (the Greek translation of the OT, often quoted by Christ and His apostles in preference to the Hebrew text) was completed.

Being born into a Jewish family in a city with this history gave Apollos enormous educational opportunities, which he grasped, growing into 'an eloquent man, and mighty in the scriptures' (18.24). Having been partially 'instructed in the way of the Lord' but 'knowing only the baptism of John', Apollos came to Ephesus 'and being fervent [*zeō*, hot] in spirit, he spake and taught diligently [*akribos*, accurately] the things of the Lord' (18.25). Unafraid and full of enthusiasm, 'he began to speak boldly in the synagogue' (18.26), probably demanding repentance, like John the Baptist.

Aquilla and Priscilla responded appropriately to Apollos' incomplete gospel preaching. Rather than publicly denounce him, they recognised his true potential, and wisely 'took him unto them, and expounded unto him the way of God more perfectly' (18.26). In doing this they showed an important function of a Christian home: the edification of young believers.

With the rise of false teachers and false brethren, it was crucial that local churches be cautious about who they received. Letters of commendation helped. Therefore, when Apollos wished to expand his sphere of ministry, being 'disposed to pass into Achaia, the brethren wrote, exhorting the disciples to receive him' (18.27). They received him, without regret, because Apollos 'helped them much which had believed through grace; for he mightily convinced the Jews, and that publickly, shewing by the scriptures that Jesus was Christ' (v28; cf. 1 Cor 3.6). Now in possession of full gospel truth, with fresh vigour Apollos proved from the Old Testament that Jesus of Nazareth, crucified, buried, and resurrected, was truly God's Anointed.

Some of the results of Apollos' incomplete gospel preaching lingered. Arriving in Ephesus, Paul discovered twelve disciples living in a kind of dispensational time-warp (19.1-7). They had not received nor even heard of the Holy Spirit, and instead of undergoing Christian baptism, had been baptised unto John's 'baptism of repentance' (19.4). As soon as Paul explained the anticipatory nature of John's message, challenging his hearers to 'believe on him which should come after him, that is, on Christ Jesus', they believed and were 'baptized in the name of the Lord Jesus' (19.4, 5). Their position was unique, as was their reception of the Spirit, mediated through the laying on of Paul's hand and confirmed by prophesying and speaking in foreign languages (19.6). The more normal Christian experience is the immediate indwelling of the Spirit of God, in all His fullness, at conversion (Eph 1.13).

Paul now began his Ephesian campaign in earnest (19.8-12), entering the synagogue and 'speaking out boldly [*parrhēsiazomai*, speak freely, without fear] for three months' (19.8, NASB). This unrestrained delivery of divine truth characterised his preaching from the beginning (9.27, 29; 13.46; 14.3; 18.26; 26.26; Eph 6.20; 1 Thess 2.2). Even though the gospel is to be proclaimed as a command from God, Paul reasoned with logic, feeling and passion, doing his utmost to persuade his Jewish hearers of the genuineness and urgency of the message 'about the kingdom of God' (v8, NASB). Like Apollos, he had to prove from the Old Testament that Jesus of Nazareth was God's Anointed, that the death of Christ and the shedding of His precious blood would ratify the New Covenant, laying the foundation for the coming Kingdom (Jer 31.31-40; 1 Cor 11.25). He needed to declare that this same Jesus had risen from the dead and ascended to heaven, from whence He will return as Israel's Messiah, King of all kings and Lord of all lords. This Kingdom message required confession that Jesus is Lord and belief that God had raised Him from the dead (Rom 10.9).

After three months preaching, 'when some were becoming hardened and disobedient, speaking evil of the Way [not just the message, but Christ Himself, Jn 14.6] before the multitude, he withdrew from them' (19.9, NASB). After prolonged Christian testimony in an area is rejected, it may be fitting to withdraw (cf. Mt 10.14). God may do it by closing a local assembly. At Ephesus Paul left the synagogue and 'took away the disciples, reasoning daily in the school of Tyrannus ... for two years' (19.9, 10, NASB). Paul's steadfast preaching was miraculously endorsed through the sweat cloths and aprons he used while labouring as a tent maker to support himself (18.3; 19.12; 20.34; cf. Heb 2.3, 4). The impact on the region was enormous: 'all they which dwelt in Asia heard the word of the Lord Jesus, both Jews and Greeks' (v10).

Imitation is one of Satan's most effective strategies. But when seven wandering Jews attempted to duplicate Paul's exorcisms, using the name of Jesus', they got more than they bargained for. The demon knew about Jesus and Paul – an amazing testimony to the effectiveness of the latter's service for God – but did not acknowledge any authority in the sons of Sceva (19.15, NASB). Instead, with supernatural strength the demoniac violently assaulted them, news of which spread throughout Ephesus, so that 'fear fell on them all, and the name of the Lord Jesus was magnified' (19.16, 17). Something else contributed to the growth of God's word. The transforming power of the gospel was seen in young converts publicly renouncing their occult practices and incinerating their expensive magic books in one great conflagration (19.18-20). Just after this, intending to revisit the believers in Macedonia and Achaia, before going to Jerusalem and then onwards to Rome, Paul 'sent into Macedonia two of them that ministered unto him, Timotheus and Erastus' (19.21, 22). While things did not work out as planned – Paul reached Rome as a prisoner, not a free man – nonetheless, his careful planning and evangelistic enthusiasm should characterise us.

Ephesus was proud of her temple of Diana (Artemis), a goddess depicted as a multi-breasted woman. It is said that the previous temple burnt down the night that Alexander the Great was born. This replacement – one of the seven wonders of the ancient world – whose immense foundations were sunk into marshland to protect it from earthquakes, was under construction when Alexander visited the city. Famously, they refused his generous offer to subsidise the rebuilding costs.[31] In Paul's day the Ephesians vaunted their pride by mindlessly chanting 'great is Diana of the Ephesians' (19.34). At that time the term *neōkoros* or 'temple sweeper', which had depicted the lowest of the goddess's servants, had become a title of honour, so that the city itself was described as 'a worshipper [*neōkoros*] of the great goddess Diana, and of the image [likely a meteor] which fell down from Jupiter' (v35).

Nothing angers a man quite as much as loss of money. This is exactly what happened to Demetrius and his silversmith colleagues. A lucrative trade in silver models of the temple (v24) was at its peak. The presence of 'certain of the chief of Asia [*Asiarchēs*]' (v31), wealthy, elected officials who sponsored public festivals and games, suggests that these games were in progress, leading to an influx of people from the surrounding area. The crowds would have swelled further because 'the courts [were] being held, and there [were] proconsuls [touring judges]' (v38, JND). As a result of Paul's preaching, so many had turned from idolatry that sales in silver shrines had fallen (vv24-27). The enraged Demetrius cleverly played on local pride in the temple to stir up his colleagues and, in turn, whip up the whole city into a frenzy (vv29-34). As Luke wrote, 'there arose no small disturbance concerning the way' (v23, NASB).

Alarmed by the effect this uproar could have on the privileges of Ephesus, the town-clerk, who carried overall responsibility for civic behaviour, endeavoured to calm the crowd (vv35-40). He emphasized that Ephesus' commitment to Diana was unchallengeable; he pointed out that the Christian missionaries had neither robbed temples nor railed against Diana; and he explained that if 'Demetrius and the artisans who [are] with him have a matter against any one, the courts are being held, and there are proconsuls' (v38, JND). Having 'thus spoken, he dismissed the assembly' (v41). In this way God protected Paul and his friends from harm.

19

EQUIPPING THE EPHESIAN ELDERS (20.1-38)

APPROXIMATELY 3,000KM IS COVERED in a few short verses, as Paul
travelled from Macedonia to Greece, around the bay of the Aegean
Sea and back (vv1-6). This area contained familiar New Testament
locations such as Philippi, Galatia, Thessalonica, Berea, Athens, and
Corinth; but Luke, under the inspiration of the Spirit, focusses on
the return via Troas (vv7-16) and, upon reaching Miletus, Paul's
stirring final address to the Ephesian elders (vv17-38).

The servant at work (vv1-6)

The traumatic riot in Ephesus prompted Paul to move on (v1).
Although the world's opposition shouldn't surprise us (Jn 16.33;
2 Tim 3.12), the two embraces between Paul and the Ephesian
disciples (vv1, 37) show that **an oasis of encouragement may be
expected among the Lord's people**.

Scant detail exists of the three months in Greece (vv2, 3) but
silence does not prove indolence for there is significant evidence
that it was during this period that Paul wrote Romans (the journey
to Jerusalem with a gift for the poor saints (v16, 24.17; Rom 15.25-
27); the 'much exhortation' delaying Paul from visiting Rome (v2;
Rom 15.19-26); and the carrier of the letter, Phebe, came from
Cenchrea, a port of Corinth (Rom 16.1). The Roman letter is a
priceless treasure of truth that will repay diligent study, prompting
Calvin's comment, 'when anyone understands this Epistle, he
has a passage opened to him to the understanding of the whole
Scripture.'[32]

Providentially, Paul learned of an ambush planned by his dogged adversaries (v3; cf. 23.16). To avoid attack, he changed his plans, returning by land instead of sea (v3). We should be thankful, for had he sailed direct to Syria, the valuable final address to the Ephesian elders could not have taken place (vv17-38). **Sensible planning and God's sovereign overruling work in harmony**.

Paul's travelling companions (v4) came in pairs from Thessalonica, Derbe, and Asia. Only Sopater came from Berea. They may have accompanied the financial gift from their company, showing interest in their Jewish brethren and a concern for financial transparency. **There is practical value in partnering in service:** pairing up provides additional safety, satisfaction, and strength (Ecc 4.9-12). It also establishes a testimony (Jn 8.17; Deut 19.15). Notably, the Lord sent His apostles out two by two (Mk 6.7).

The group went ahead to Troas, while Paul and Luke ('us', v5) remained in Philippi. Perhaps Paul, aware that **seasonal opportunities arise** (2 Tim 4.2), used the 'days of unleavened bread' (v6) to preach Christ from the Jewish feasts. Certainly, he taught the nearby Corinthians that Christ's death provided *redemption* like the Passover (1 Cor 5.7); just as homes were to be leaven-free in the ensuing week, the Christian life is to be marked by *separation* from sin (1 Cor 5.6-8); and the resurrection of Christ is like the Feast of First Fruits, setting the *expectation* of a greater harvest to come (1 Cor 15.20). Luke noted that the descent of the Holy Spirit fulfilled the day of Pentecost (2.1), and perhaps the joyful *liberation* associated with this feast (Deut 16.9-12) prefigured the similar ministry of the Holy Spirit (Rom 8.2-6). Significantly, the remaining annual feasts (Trumpets, Day of Atonement, Tabernacles) are yet to be fulfilled.

Luke records various travel durations: five days from Philippi to Troas (v6); three days from Miletus to Troas (v15); an effort to get to Jerusalem by the day of Pentecost (v16), allowing fifty days overall between Philippi and Jerusalem (cf. Deut 16.9 – the Feast of Weeks, i.e., Pentecost, was seven weeks after the Feast of First Fruits, for which they were in Philippi, v6). These journeys were difficult and dangerous (2 Cor 11.26). Paul gave up comfort, embracing hardship for the sake of Christ's name, and similarly urged Timothy to 'endure hardness' (2 Tim 2.3), for **pioneering evangelism is not easy**.

The week in Troas (vv7-12)

Here we have a heart-warming snapshot of life in an early church. Notice that **they met regularly**, gathering on the first day of the week (v7). This is the most basic feature of a church and responsibility of fellowship for the word church (*ekklēsía*) means an assembling of people (cf. 19.32).

They **broke bread regularly** each first day of the week (v7), not the first day of the month, or quarter, or year. There is profound value in Christ's simple command to remember Him (1 Cor 11.23-24). It involves contemplating His person and work (1 Cor 11.24-25), a transforming exercise (2 Cor 3.18). Anticipating His return (1 Cor 11.26) is purifying (1 Jn 3.3); considering other believers (1 Cor 11.33) is uniting (1 Jn 5.1); and judging personal sin (1 Cor 11.28-32) is vitalising (Rom 8.13).

They **had a distinct identity**. Israel was commanded to observe the seventh day (Ex 20.10-11; 31.7), but the church is not Israel (1 Cor 10.32 distinguishes between Jew, Gentile, and church of God); rather, it is a new body containing both believing Jews and Gentiles (Eph 2.11-15). The vital link between the church and her exalted head (Eph 5.23) is fittingly expressed by the new meeting–day - the day He rose from the dead (Mt 28.1; Jn 20.19). This also became the day for worshipful giving (1 Cor 16.2).

There **was an interest in God's word**. Capitalising on Paul's presence, the preaching continued until midnight (v7), although we should recall that being a working day, the meeting likely started in the evening. Paul 'discoursed' (vv7, 9 Derby, Weymouth), suggesting questions were put to him and answered, on what may well have been their final opportunity to do so (cf. v38). We too should grasp opportunities to acquire spiritual riches.

The young were there. Luke uses two words to describe Eutychus' youthfulness: *neanías* (v9) and *país* (v12). The first can be used of a young man (7.58), the second of children ranging from under two years (Mt 2.16) up to twelve years of age (Lk 8.42,54). This makes it hard to age Eutychus precisely. The young may struggle to concentrate during the exposition of scripture, but there is no better place for them to be than where God's word, simultaneously milk for the new-born (1 Pet 2.2) and meat for the mature (Heb 5.12-14), is taught.

The buildings were basic. Nothing more than an 'upper chamber' on the third floor of an undescribed building was required (vv8, 9). Functional buildings may be convenient, but fancy architecture adds nothing to true worship, which is spiritual in character (Jn 4.23-24). The early church frequently met in homes (Rom 16.4; Philem 2). The true building work is what God does in His people's lives (1 Pet 2.5).

It was not a secret society. The church met with lights on and windows open (v8, 9). Doubtless this aided ventilation, but there is an important point here. Christ's doctrine was spoken openly to the world (Jn 18.20-21). Paul envisaged unbelievers entering church gatherings to observe what was going on (1 Cor 14.23-25). There is nothing to hide when we 'preach the word'.

They witnessed the power of God. If it were not for Luke's record (who, as a doctor, was qualified to comment) that Eutychus was 'taken up dead' (v9), we might well wonder whether his restoration to life after falling out a third-floor window was really a miracle?

Paul's calm words of comfort (v10) parallel the Lord's words when He raised Jairus' daughter (Lk 8.52); in both cases the priority appears to have been avoiding unhelpful publicity for the child. Miracles like this were foundational signs from God, confirming the Apostle's testimony to Christ (Heb 2.4). The apostolic foundation being now laid, they are no longer needed (Eph 2.20); nonetheless God's power is still witnessed in the church through sinners being saved (Rom 1.16), sanctified (Jn 17.17), and sustained (1 Pet 1.5).

They sorrowed and rejoiced together. When Eutychus fell, the assembly was 'troubled' (v10, also translated 'making a noise' Mt 9.23, or 'ado' Mk 5.39). When he was brought back upstairs, they 'were not a little comforted' (v12). This assembly felt each other's sorrow and joy in unison, living out the truth of being a vitally linked together body (Rom 12.15).

Following Eutychus' restoration, the assembly reconvened on the third floor to converse (v11) and break bread, (that is, to eat a common meal[33]). In this assembly **they ate and talked together.** Over time, sadly, the feasts associated with the Lord's supper (2.42, 46; Jude 12) caused divisions, prompting Paul to urge satisfying hunger at home, prior to gathering (1 Cor 11.20-21, 34). However, we should still at other times engage in this family-like activity (Deut 6.7; Ps 128.3b; 1 Jn 5.1), enriching our fellowship.

Paul's journey to Assos (vv13-16)

After the eventful all-night meeting in Troas, Paul journeyed alone by foot to Assos while Luke and the rest of the group went by ship ('we', v13), showing that **times of solitude are necessary.** This gave him the opportunity to prepare his important final counsel to the Ephesian elders. If we are to say things of value in public, we must prioritise time with God and His word in private (v32). Paul evidently felt free to temporarily leave the group, pointing to a mutual respect for each other's individual will (cf. 15.34; 1 Cor 16.12). This is a natural extension of the truth that each of us is directly accountable to the Lord (Rom 14.4). Reference to a map shows that Paul's chosen walking route was easy for the ship to accommodate, pointing to a beautiful consideration in his planning. He was not selfishly pulling rank, but taking an opportunity that did not significantly inconvenience the group. Paul's opportunistic physical exercise is a reminder that our bodies are neither to be idolised or despised. They are to be cared for (1 Tim 4.8).

Paul's farewell address to the Ephesian elders (vv17-38)

Paul's remarks here provide an abiding pattern for the sustainability of an assembly, after the pioneering missionary has gone. To navigate the dangers that lay ahead, he urged them to remember what he had taught them.

Two features stand out in **Paul's bond-service to Christ** (vv18-19). The first is *consistency*. He appealed to their knowledge of him 'at all seasons' (v18), a period spanning three years (v31) and including a variety of trials (v19). Steadfast continuance is one of the greatest tests of reality (2.42; 11.23). Secondly, he served with *humility* of mind (v19); an attitude that, he taught elsewhere, contrasts with strife, vainglory, and despising others (Phil 2.3). Clearly, the unselfish mindset that pursues peace instead of making trouble, that prioritises Christ's glory over its own, and esteems others better than itself, is indispensable to the peaceful progress of any relationship and any local church.

We may form an ABCDE from **Paul's approach to preaching** (vv20-21, 27). It was *adaptable*, for he preached 'publicly' (v20), an efficient way to edify many; but also privately, 'from house to house' (v20). Like the Master, he had time for individuals. His preaching was *beneficial* as he sought to impart spiritual riches to his hearers and left out 'nothing that was profitable' (v20, cf. Rom 1.11, Eph 3.8). It was *comprehensive*; he had 'not shunned to declare…all the counsel of God' ('not shunned' v27, and 'kept back' v20, are both *hupostéllō*). The uncomfortable and unpopular parts of God's word must be proclaimed. It was *demanding*, for he taught by example ('showed' v20), as well as exhortation ('taught' v20, cf. 1.1; Ezra 7.10). The three-year period with the Ephesians (v31) provided ample opportunity to observe the correlation between Paul's lip and his life.

Paul's preaching was *extensive*, for he made clear God's terms for Jew and Gentile sinners to be made right with Him: 'repentance… and faith' (v21). With first-hand experience of the lavish kindness of God, he testified to 'the gospel of the grace of God' (v24). His message embraced 'the kingdom of God' (v25), since our response to the gospel determines our relationship to the Kingdom that Christ will establish at His second coming. Those who do not believe will not see it (Jn 3.3) and will instead be banished to a place of torment (Mt 13.49-50; Rev 20.11-15). Those who do believe will, after the trials of this life, enter and participate in the long anticipated, literal kingdom of God (14.22; 2 Tim 2.12). This monumental truth is disclosed in the Scriptures as an incentive to perseverance and faithfulness.

To replicate what Paul did with the Ephesians, consecutive exposition by local teaching brethren has much to commend it.

Paul's exemplary commitment (vv22-27) is seen in his choice of five lively metaphors, each revealing wholehearted devotion to Christ. As an *accountant*, Paul had done the sums (v24): to lose his life in the service of Christ was a price worth paying. This is a humbling reminder that it is not possible to sacrifice too much in the service of the One who gave Himself for us. As a *runner*, Paul wanted to finish his 'course with joy' (v24); not content with simply passing the finish line, Paul wanted believers to run the race well (1 Cor 9.24; Gal 5.7; cf. Heb 12.1). His responsibility as a *witness* was solemnly to testify to the gospel of the grace of God (v21, 24). Paul repeatedly recounted his dramatic encounter with the risen Lord Jesus, making him the last resurrection eyewitness, and radically transforming him from chief persecutor to chief preacher of the gospel (1 Cor 15.5-8). Paul preached as a *herald* (v25, *kērússō*) representing the king, since the gospel is a formal announcement from God to be obeyed (1 Pet 4.11,17). Lastly, Paul's claim to be 'pure from the blood of all men' (v26) echoes God's description of Ezekiel as a *watchman* (Eze 3.16-21; 33.7-9). Ezekiel's duty was to warn the wicked and any erring righteous of the consequences of their ways. He was not culpable for their response, only for passing the message on. Gospel preaching is solemn.

Like the Lord (Mt 13.37-43), **Paul forewarned of harmful infiltrators** (vv28-32). He prepared the Ephesians with *a call to duty* (v28). First, they were to maintain a careful self-scrutiny, a basic duty of every Christian (Eph 5.15). Second, they were to maintain an all-inclusive flock-watch. The order is significant: looking out for others but not myself is a recipe for hypocrisy (Mt 7.3-5); further, an awareness of personal frailty is exactly what is needed to help others in trouble (Gal 6.1). Third, they were to 'feed, [as a shepherd] the church of God'. The spiritual shepherd is concerned that the flock grazes in the good pasture of the word of God. Fourth, they were to appreciate the preciousness of the flock. The church is 'purchased with the blood of His Own' (JND), a term expressing nearness of relationship and thus the dearness of the Lord Jesus to the Father. The value of a local church is not proportional to its size, but to the currency of its redemption, which is infinite.

Next Paul gave **a warning of danger** (vv29-30) for he knew that after his departure 'grievous wolves' would enter (cf. Moses, Deut 31.29). Shortly, Jude would confirm that 'there are certain men crept in unawares' (Jude 4), men who perverted grace, making it a free ticket to sin. Another source of danger would sadly come from within. In the pursuit of popularity, some would speak 'perverse [distorted] things'. Paul similarly warned Timothy, 'the time will come when they will not endure sound doctrine; but after their own lusts shall they heap to themselves teachers, having itching ears; and they shall turn away their ears from the truth' (2 Tim 4.3-4). Preaching must conform to the unchanging word of God, not the current public mood.

With threats in every direction, Paul reminded them of their **sufficient defence** (v31, 32). He stressed again that they had to 'watch'; since a failure in basic vigilance has caused the best soldiers to be easily defeated (2 Sam 20.10). Second, they had to 'remember' all Paul had taught them. Oral instruction etches itself into the memory, and the godly counsel of those who have taught us the word of God ought to be cherished and pondered (Heb 13.7). Third, there is 'God'. Within a few years Paul would be dead, but God alone is the great sustainer of His people, and it is on Him we must rely. Finally, 'the word of His grace,' which contains all that is required for spiritual stability, means we can face the unknown, alert but not alarmed.

Paul's financial arrangements (vv33-35) were exemplary. He was *content* with what he had, for he 'coveted no man's silver, or gold, or apparel' (v33), and worked to meet his 'necessities' (v34) rather than provide himself with luxuries. Paul was *diligent*, because the money he did possess was acquired through the graft of his own hands (v34), and sometimes involved 'labouring' to the point of weariness (v35, *'kopiaō'*). That Paul was *benevolent* is demonstrated by his financial support for those who served with him, and the weak who could not work to support themselves. His motivation was to prove the Lord's promise, a promise not recorded in the Gospels but revealed here: 'it is more blessed to give than to receive' (v35). This example provides a balanced attitude toward secular employment: we work diligently to meet our needs, to support our service for the Lord, to support those serving around us, to support those in a position of need, to experience the joy of giving. Elsewhere Paul gratefully acknowledged those who supported him in his gospel missions (Phil 4.15); and asserted the right of the gospel preacher to be supported for his spiritual labours (1 Cor 9.14). But when it came to the model he held out for general imitation, he promoted a blend of secular and spiritual labour - a course that avoided burdening the saints and didn't give a stick to his many opponents to beat him with (2 Thess 3.8-9; 2 Cor 11.7-12).

Prior to their emotional final parting (vv36-38) they prayed together. Paul left the Ephesians with the same resources we have today: may we prove the all-sufficiency of 'God and…the word of His grace' as we navigate all that lies on the way to the finishing line.

20

PAUL'S FINAL JOURNEY TO JERUSALEM (21.1-17)

This section completes Paul's third missionary journey and records his final voyage to Jerusalem. Yearning after his Jewish brothers, keen to be at Jerusalem for Pentecost, and determined to bring a gift to the local Christians, Paul felt 'bound in the spirit' to go (20.16, 22; 24.17; Rom 9.2, 3, 15.25-31; 1 Cor 16.1-6). And yet, as he approached the capital, he was repeatedly cautioned that danger awaited him (20.22, 23; 21.4, 11). Rather than being divine prohibitions, these Spirit-inspired alerts seem to have been simple warnings of what was to come. After all, to be forewarned is to be forearmed.

Paul and his companions were so fond of the Ephesian elders, they had to tear themselves from them (v1).[34] Departing from Miletus, they sailed to Koos, 'the day following to Rhodes, and from thence to Patara' (v1). Leaving Patara, they sailed to Tyre, 'for there the ship was to unlade her burden' (v2, 3). In Tyre, Paul and his friends sought out fellow believers, some of whom may have escaped to that region at the time of Stephen's stoning (8.1; 11.19). After only seven days, during which the brethren counselled Paul through the Spirit not to go to Jerusalem, they felt such a strong mutual Christian connection that whole families accompanied Paul's group to the seashore, where they kneeled and prayed together (vv4, 5). During a stop-off at Ptolemais, the missionary group 'saluted the brethren, and abode with them one day' (v7).

The next day, Paul travelled to Caesarea, where he stayed with Philip the evangelist. Twenty years had now passed since Philip, having led the Ethiopian eunuch to Christ, had evangelized Azotus and 'preached in all the cities, till he came to Caesarea' (8.40). In that city, he had settled and raised a family for God, so that all four of his daughters were saved, morally pure, and spiritually gifted (v9). But God did not use them to deliver a prophetic word to Paul. Instead, He brought Agabus, who had previously foreseen the Jerusalem famine (11.28), from Judaea to Caesarea to predict Paul's imprisonment (vv10, 11). Everyone present was genuinely concerned for his welfare. However, when he asserted that he was fully steeled not only for bondage but death 'at Jerusalem for the name of the Lord Jesus', they stopped trying to dissuade him, saying 'The will of the Lord be done' (vv12-14). In the face of inevitable suffering, this fortitude mirrored Christ's Own resolve 'to go to Jerusalem', knowing all that would befall Him there (Lk 9.51). After those few days at Caesarea, accompanied by his friends, some of the Caesarean disciples and Mnason, a mature Cypriot Christian with whom they would lodge, Paul went the last few miles to Jerusalem (vv15, 16).

PART 3

PAUL'S ARREST, IMPRISONMENT, AND JOURNEY TO ROME
(21.17-28.31)

ARRIVING AT JERUSALEM, Paul and his companions were warmly received by the Christians. When he met James and the other elders, Paul detailed 'what things God had wrought among the Gentiles by his ministry' (21.17-19). As well as delivering this accurate, humble, and God-glorifying report, Paul probably handed over a substantial gift diligently collected from Gentile churches for the poor Jerusalem saints (cf. 24.17; Rom 15.25-31; 1 Cor 16.1-6).

Luke did not mention the gift. Instead, he focused on James and his fellow elders' concern regarding the Jews' criticism of Paul. They had heard that thousands of believing Jews who remained zealous for the Law of Moses believed that Paul taught Jews to forsake the Law, abandon Jewish customs, and stop circumcising their children (21.20, 21). These rumours were a gross misrepresentation of his ministry. At Antioch, Paul had opposed those who insisted converted Gentiles be circumcised (15.1, 2). He even wrote to the Galatians that 'in Jesus Christ neither circumcision availeth any thing, nor uncircumcision; but faith which worketh by love' (Gal 5.6). But while Paul taught Jews that neither circumcision nor legal obedience could justify or sanctify, it is never recorded that he forbade Jews to practise these things as a matter of conscience. During his second missionary journey, to avoid any needless insult to local Jews, he went so far as to have Timothy circumcised (16.3). As he wrote to the Corinthians, 'unto the Jews I became as a Jew, that I might gain the Jews; to them that are under the law, as under the law, that I might gain them that are under the law' (1 Cor 9.20).

Desiring to scotch further offence and refute the allegations against Paul, James and the others suggested he purify himself by paying for the sacrifices of four men under a vow. Given that this oath included head-shaving and a ritual seven-day cleansing in the temple, it was probably a Nazarite vow (21.22-24; cf. Num 6.1-12). In case Paul had any doubts, James and his fellow elders reassured him that Gentile converts should not be subjected to the same legal requirements; they need only shun 'things offered to idols, and from blood, and from strangled, and from fornication' (21.25).

At this distance – temporally, culturally, and spatially – it is difficult to know if it was the right thing to do. Luke passes no judgment. Nevertheless, Paul acquiesced to James' suggestion, entered the temple, identified himself with the four men, and paid for their sacrifices (21.24, 26). In so doing he precipitated his arrest. Near the end of the seven-day ceremony, Jews from Asia Minor spotted Paul, stirred up the people, seized him, and cried out, 'Men of Israel, help: This is the man, that teacheth all *men* everywhere against the people, and the law, and this place: and further brought Greeks also into the temple, and hath polluted this holy place' (21.27, 28). Having seen Paul in Jerusalem with his Ephesian travelling companion Trophimus, they wrongly assumed that Paul had brought him into the temple (20.4; 21.29). As they forcibly ejected Paul from the Court of the Women, slammed shut the doors of the Beautiful Gate, and 'went about to kill him', it must have felt as though the whole city had turned against him (21.30, 31).

Fort Antonio overlooked the temple courts. As soon as Claudius Lysius the chief captain heard of the commotion, he and his soldiers rushed into the temple complex (21.31, 32; cf. 23.26). Had he delayed, Paul would have been killed. God thus used a Gentile tribune to save His servant's life. The chief captain's immediate assumption was that Paul was a false Egyptian prophet who had led four hundred assassins into the wilderness[1] (21.38). Determined to get to the bottom of the trouble, he had Paul chained (21.33). When this failed, he commanded that Paul 'be carried into the castle' (21.33, 34). The Jews were so fired up, they chased the soldiers, 'crying, Away with him' (21.35, 36). This echoed Israel's words to Pilate about Christ: 'Away with *him*, away with *him*, crucify him' (Jn 19.15). While the Lord Jesus went quietly, 'as a lamb to the slaughter, and as a sheep before her shearers is dumb, so he [opened] not his mouth' (Is 53.7), Paul asked permission to address the crowd (21.37, 39).

Without hesitation, Paul switched from speaking Greek to Claudius Lysias to Hebrew to the Jewish crowd. His gusto and charisma, together with his Hebrew fluency, silenced the angry mob (21.40; 22.1, 2). He told them of his birth into a Jewish family in the respected Cilician university city of Tarsus and his tutelage in Jerusalem 'at the feet of Gamaliel', the greatest living Jewish teacher (22.3). In his misdirected zeal for God, he had hunted down Christians, intending to imprison and kill them (22.3, 4). If asked, Israel's religious leaders could verify his past hatred for Christ's followers, because they had authorized his visit 'to Damascus, to bring them which were there bound unto Jerusalem, for to be punished' (22.5).

But in a flash his life changed. As he approached Damascus, at about noon a dazzling, heavenly light shone round about him (22.6). His companions saw a bright, terrifying light and heard an indistinct noise (22.9; cf. 9.7; Dan 10.6). Saul fell to the ground, hearing the voice of the resurrected, exalted Jesus of Nazareth, Whose followers he had been maltreating, ask, 'Saul, Saul, why persecutest thou me?' (22.7, 8). The proud Pharisee humbly requested direction from the Lord of glory (22.10). As he was obeying the first command, to enter Damascus, Ananias, a devout Jewish believer, was receiving the Lord's instruction to lay his hands on this monstrous tormenter of the church. This he did, saying, 'Brother Saul, receive thy sight' (22.10-13). Immediately, his eyes were opened. Ananias then explained that the God of his forefathers had chosen him to know His will (personally, and ecclesiastically), see the Just One, hear God's voice, tell everyone of what he had 'seen and heard', and (picturing the washing away of his sins when he called on the Lord) be baptised (22.14-16; cf. Eph 3.2-13).

Three years later, Paul returned to Jerusalem, but because the Jews would not receive his testimony, and in any case he was to be sent to the Gentiles, the Lord told him to flee (22.18-21; cf. Gal 1.18). This was the crisis moment. As soon as he uttered the word 'Gentiles', his Jewish audience exploded. Demanding his death, they disrobed 'and threw dust into the air' (22.22, 23). Utterly perplexed by their fury, Claudius Lysias commanded Paul to be taken to the castle and 'examined by scourging' (22.24). 'Consisting of leather thongs, weighted with rough pieces of metal or bone, and attached to a stout wooden handle'[2], the Roman scourge (Latin *flagellum*) was a fearsome device, from which Roman citizens were protected. With one question, Paul saved himself from its lacerations: 'Is it lawful for you to scourge a man that is a Roman, and uncondemned?' (22.25). As soon as Claudius Lysias learned that Paul was a freeborn Roman citizen, he knew he had to tread carefully (22.27, 28). Even Paul's binding was a cardinal offence (22.29).

The next day, Paul was set before the Jewish Sanhedrin (22.30). Unfazed by the highest religious council in the land and unashamed of his arrest, Paul claimed to 'have lived in all good conscience before God until [that] day' (23.1). With his whole life, pre- and post-conversion, having been totally committed to God, he was as good a Jew as any of them (24.16; 26.4, 5; cf. 2 Cor 1.12; 2.17; 4.2; Phil 3.4-6). As soon as Paul spoke, Ananias, the ruthless, unprincipled, and greedy high priest who 'seized for himself the tithes that ought to have gone to the common priests,'[3] ordered that they punch him on the mouth (23.2; cf. Jn 18.22, 23). However, Paul was not easily cowed. Sharp-witted and gutsy, he countered, 'God shall smite thee, thou whited wall: for sittest thou to judge me after the law, and commandest me to be smitten contrary to the law?' (23.3). Essentially, he was condemning Ananias for gross hypocrisy, of being a cracked and rickety wall whose flaws were concealed by a liberal application of whitewash (cf. Eze 13.11; Mt 23.27). Paul's words proved prophetic. In AD 58-59, Ananias was dismissed from office. In AD 66, Jewish guerrillas assassinated him as a pro-Roman.[4] In this way, God smote the 'whited wall'!

Those who stood by accused Paul of vilifying God's high priest (23.4). Confessing he had not realised that the brutish Ananias was the high priest, Paul conceded that Moses forbade the maligning of rulers (20.5). John Phillips suggests that Paul would not have recognised Ananias and, because of the unplanned nature of this meeting, Ananias might not have been 'arrayed in his official robes.'[5] Perceiving a natural rift in the council between the Pharisees, who believed in a resurrection and angels, and the Sadducees, who denied both, and knowing full well that he would not receive a fair trial, Paul cried out, 'Men and brethren, I am a Pharisee, the son of a Pharisee: of the hope and resurrection of the dead I am called in question' (23.6; cf. 26.6-8). With these few carefully chosen words, he destabilised the entire Sanhedrin. The Pharisees sided with Paul, the Sadducees resisted, and chaos ensued. Yet again, Claudius Lysias was forced to rescue Paul and take him to the castle (23.7-10).

That night the Lord appeared to Paul, firmly assuring him, 'as thou hast testified of me in Jerusalem, so must thou bear witness also at Rome' (23.11). It was impossible, therefore, that these Jerusalem Jews could kill him, even though at first light more than forty swore they would neither eat nor drink till they had assassinated Paul (23.12, 13). Even though it was a ridiculous oath, born out of misplaced passion and probably a pathetic attempt to court Ananias' favour, the chief priests and elders were happy for them to give it a go (23.14, 15; cf. Isa 1.21).

Yet again, God overruled so that Paul's nephew caught wind of the plot (23.16). He reported it to Paul, who requested that one of the centurions take his young nephew to Claudius Lysias (23.17, 18). When he, with the utmost discretion, heard of the conspiracy, he knew he had a serious problem (23.19-22). By this stage, he understood the Jews' accusations were religious, not civil and that Paul had done nothing deserving of execution or imprisonment (23.29). Furthermore, because Paul was a Roman citizen, his future was now inextricably linked with Paul's. If Paul died in his custody, he was accountable. In a moment, he decided to get rid of Paul. Having Rome's military machine at his disposal, Clausius Lysias commanded two centurions to prepare two hundred soldiers, seventy cavalry, and two hundred spearmen, to take Paul that very night to Felix at Caesarea Maritima (23.23, 24). By morning they had covered the thirty-five miles to Antipatris (modern-day Tel Afek); the seventy horsemen then continued with Paul the remaining twenty-seven miles to Caesarea (23.31-33).

Within two days, Claudius Lysias had handed Paul over to someone else. In his letter, he flattered Governor Felix, falsely claiming to have saved Paul because he knew he was a Roman citizen (23.25-27). On learning that Paul came from Cilicia, Felix agreed to hear his case before his accusers (23.33-35).

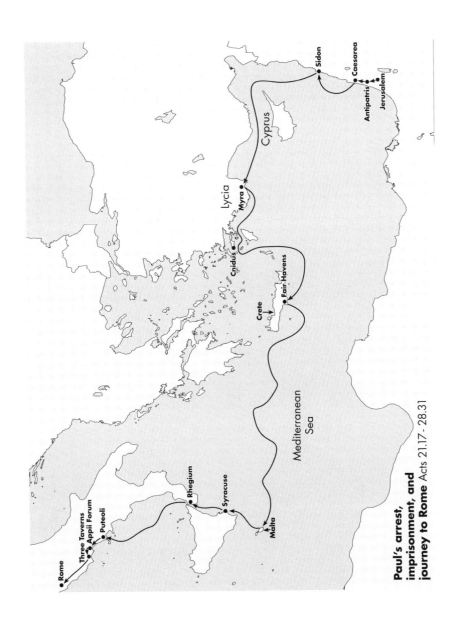

Paul's arrest, imprisonment, and journey to Rome Acts 21.17 - 28.31

21

PAUL BEFORE FELIX (24)

IN THE PROVIDENCE OF GOD, Paul's trials took him to Rome, the centre of the empire (23.11). *En route*, he witnessed to kings and governors (9.15). Felix had read Claudius Lysias' letter (23.26-30) and although the facts had been embellished, it was still in Paul's favour. The issue at stake was religious, not civil law (23.29). Ordinarily, Paul would have been exonerated, but the Jews were determined to nail him. Happy to run roughshod over justice – as they had done about thirty years earlier, when they accused the Lord Jesus of blasphemy and treason (Lk 23.2) – the Jews pushed for Paul's execution. Paul ought to have been released (24.26, 27; 25.10, 26; 26.31). But God providentially used the wicked resolve of the Jews to ensure Paul was taken to Rome, where he would preach Christ to the emperor himself (cf. 27.24; 2 Tim 4.16,17).

Prosecution (vv1-9)

Tertullus (likely a Roman) was a forensic orator who acted as a legal advocate for the Sanhedrin, the religious juggernaut which now stood 'against Paul' (v1). Having sought to tear him limb from limb and assassinate him in the shadows, they now bludgeoned him with the legal system. Although Paul was like a sheep among wolves, the Lord Jesus had promised, 'blessed are ye, when men shall ... persecute you, and shall say all manner of evil against you falsely, for my sake ... I will give you a mouth and wisdom, which all your adversaries shall not be able to gainsay' (Mt 5.11, Lk 21.15). Tertullus' opening accusation was laden with brazen flattery (vv2-4).

According to history, Felix 'exercised ... the royal prerogative in a slavish sense, with all manner of cruelties and excesses'[6]. The 'providence' of Felix, to which Tertullus referred was a peace built on bloodshed (v2). Felix had brutally crucified hundreds of rebels and overseen the assassination of Jonathan the high priest[7]. Tertullus accused Paul of being the following:

a)   A pestilent (lit. a plague) fellow, stirring up insurrection (v5a)
b)   A heretical Nazarene ringleader (lit. a front-rank man) (v5b)
c)   A flagrant temple-defiler (v6)

Charge a) was an exaggerated, vague, and irrelevant slander. Again, the Jews were trying to paint Paul as an insurrectionist, a crime which carried the death penalty. In reality, he never fomented rebellion against Rome. The offence of the cross convicted sinners – it was Paul's enemies who started revolts. Paul had been 'Plotted against at Damascus, plotted against at Jerusalem, expelled from Pisidian Antioch, stoned at Lystra, scourged and imprisoned at Philippi, accused of treason at Thessalonica, haled before the proconsul at Corinth, cause of a serious riot at Ephesus, and now finally of a riot at Jerusalem'[8]. Of course, suffering was an essential aspect of the apostolic ministry which furthered the name of Christ (9.16). As Paul wrote to the Corinthians, 'God hath set forth us the apostles last, as it were appointed to death: for we are made a spectacle unto the world ... we are fools for Christ's sake' (1 Cor 4.10).

Accusation b) 'linked Paul with Messianic movements; and the Romans knew what havoc false Messiahs could cause and how they could whip the people into hysteria which were only settled at the cost of blood.'[9] Luke refers to messianic zealots who had, in the name of religion, sought to usurp Roman rule (5.36,37; 21.38). Tertullus called Paul the chief of a fringe religious group known as the Nazarenes. This aimed at smearing him as a religious fanatic, who posed a threat to law and order. This too was vague and unproven.

Complaint c) looks back several chapters to a lie designed to stir up the Jews (21.27-29). Tertullus used it because 'Rome had given the Jews the right to execute temple desecrators.'[10] A mere supposition (21.29) was now affirmed as truth, that Paul had 'attempted to profane the temple' (24.6, JND). 'Attempted' is a highly ambiguous charge. The Jews should have dealt in actuals not speculative hypotheticals.

The Jewish prosecution combined flattery, half-truths, character assassination, and ambiguity. Although it sounded impressive, it was bereft of hard evidence, and should have been thrown out of court. Much opposition to the gospel amounts to this. In its varied forms it is fundamentally a rejection of truth. Paul was outnumbered, but in his defence he only needed to stand for the truth (cf. 2 Cor 13.8). He would not lower himself to the standards of his enemies. His words and conduct exuded veracity.

Defence (vv10 – 21)

Paul rebuffed the accusations in order, answering the charges of sedition (24.11-13), heresy (24.14-15), and temple desecration (24.17-20). Having waited silently until permitted to speak (24.10), the apostle showed self-control and dignity. In the providence of God, Felix was no judicial novice (like Lysias) but an experienced assessor of Jewish issues, meaning he would not cave to Jewish pressure.

Contrary to Tertullus' vague accusations, Paul pointed to concrete evidence. The twelve days that had elapsed since his entrance into the Jerusalem temple showed that these events were recent and, therefore, verifiable (24.11). Far from inciting rebellion, Paul said little in Jerusalem. Rather, he had entered the temple as a quiet worshipper, not a stirrer of revolt (24.12). The exaggerated claim of world-wide insurrection was sunk when Paul specified real places (e.g. synagogues and cities across the empire) where all had remained calm. Definitive truth always trumps ambiguity.

Although Tertullus had smeared 'the Way'– 'a common expression in the Acts for the Christian religion, "the characteristic direction of life as determined by faith on Jesus Christ"'[11] – Paul showed that its beliefs were perfectly orthodox, and in full accord with Old Testament teaching. People have tried to drive a wedge between the Old and the New Testament, but the apostle believed 'all things written in the law and prophets' (24.14). So should we. In aligning himself with the Old Testament, Paul came under the protection of Rome, which allowed religious freedom in conquered nations. They were suspicious of novelty but tolerated historic Judaism.

Judaism was not, however, an end in itself. Therefore, Paul proceeded to speak of the hope of the resurrection, the heart of his defence (24.15, 21b). Now answering his charge in a legal setting, he did not, at this point, explicitly mention Christ's resurrection. If he could establish that resurrection was an accepted doctrine in principle, then he could apply it to Christ's resurrection (25.19, 26.13). However, before specifically defending the Lord's resurrection, Paul used the Old Testament to defend resurrection generally.

In pointing to a resurrection of the just and unjust (24.15), Paul reminded his audience that their actions would be judged. He did not need to take justice into his own hands. As he wrote to the Romans, 'avenge not yourselves … vengeance is mine; I will repay, saith the Lord' (Rom 12.19).

The truth of the resurrection had practical implications for Paul: 'for this cause I also exercise myself to have in everything a conscience without offence towards God and men' (24.16, JND).

Unlike the prosecution, resurrection compelled Paul to speak the whole truth, and nothing but the truth. While moral integrity did not count as hard evidence *per se*, it spoke volumes to an onlooking judge. Just as wisdom cries in 'the chief places of concourse' (Pr 1.21), Paul's honesty resonated with Felix.

Paul refuted the third accusation of defiling the temple by saying that the Jews had discovered him as a purified worshipper (24.18), not a sinister temple-defiler, as they slanderously alleged. Years away from Jerusalem, had fostered sentiments of piety, not profanity (24.17). Paul stated, ironically, that although those who had found him in the Jerusalem temple had much to say in Jerusalem, in the cold light of a courtroom, when solid evidence was needed, they were conspicuously absent (24.19). 'Roman law imposed heavy penalties upon accusers who abandoned their charges, and the disappearance of accusers often meant the withdrawal of a charge. Their absence, therefore, suggested that they had nothing against him that would stand up in a Roman court of law.'[12] If a man cannot stand by his word, he is not worth listening to.

Court adjourned (vv22 – 27)

Felix should have thrown the case out, but he deferred it until Lysias arrived. In another stroke of providence, Felix was well informed of 'the Way' (24.22), which meant that he could see through the holes in the prosecution's argument. It is hard to tell what exactly motivated Felix to defer judgment. It may have been a desire to be bribed (24.26), or to follow political expediency (24.27), or simply out of curiosity (24.24). Behind the scenes, God was moving his servant to Rome. While doing so, He ensured Paul enjoyed relative liberty (24.23).

Providentially, Felix had a Jewish wife in the vicinity. Drusilla, the daughter of Herod Agrippa I (like another Herod, Lk 23.8) seemed to have some interest in 'the Way'. In preaching righteousness (24.25), Paul exposed this couple's sins. Self-control addressed their utter impotence to overcome the power of their sinful nature. Coming judgment reminded them of the consequence of sin (the root), and sins (the fruit). Far from indulging their inquisitiveness, Paul challenged their consciences. Similarly, every preacher must apply the sword of God's word to the hearts of men. Because Felix and Drusilla were living in adultery, they needed to be warned of coming judgement. 'Drusilla's brother Agrippa II gave her in marriage to the king of Emesa … but when she was still only sixteen, Felix persuaded her … to leave her husband and marry him.'[13] No wonder Paul's reasoning caused Felix to tremble. Men need to learn that there is a God 'with whom [they have] to do' (Heb 4.13).

Unfortunately, Felix delayed, and dismissed Paul (24.25). His growing interest in money, also made subsequent conversations less profitable (24.26). Paul had a clear conscience in public and private, meaning he would not bribe Felix. The message he preached rested on his personal integrity. He had come to Jerusalem to give charity to poor saints, not to line a governor's pockets. Refusing to compromise, Paul was willing to 'endure hardness, as a good soldier of Jesus Christ' (2 Tim 2.3).

For two years unrepentant Felix wrongfully held Paul. The Lord replaced him with Festus. Paul's wrongful captivity is depressing from a human point of view, but ultimately the arrival of Festus would move Paul further to Rome. What man means for evil God works for good. The governing authorities may have been set again Paul, but 'if God be for us, who can be against us?' (Rom 8.31).

22

FESTUS AND THE JEWS (25.1-12)

In Jerusalem (vv1-5)

Porcius Festus entered his new procuratorship as the head of the province of Syria. 'Judea was not strictly a province, but a department of the province of Syria.'[14] The provincial capital of Syria and centre of Roman administration was Caesarea. Although Festus hurried to Jerusalem to meet with the religious leaders and heal the diplomatic ties severed by Felix, he would ultimately try Paul in Caesarea. Felix had been summoned to Rome, to face charges for his tumultuous rule. He would have been severely punished had his brother Pallas (secretary to the emperor) not interceded on his behalf.[15]

Festus was more politically stable than Felix, and acted with conscientious efficiency (cf. 25.1, 4, 6, 12, 17, 22). However, as soon as Festus set foot in Jerusalem the Jews had only one thing in mind – to murder Paul (25.2, cf. 25.15). Although two years had elapsed, and with it a change of high priest,[16] their malice remained unabated. They 'laid legal and formal information against Paul' (25.2 Wuest, cf. 25.15) and 'kept on begging (Festus) … all the while preparing an ambush' (25.3, Wuest) to kill Paul. They desired a 'favour' (*charis* – grace) from Festus but were utterly bereft of any themselves. The religious class of AD 59 were no different to the class of AD 32; they were of their 'father the devil' (Jn 8.44) - murderers. Religious systems are always opposed to the godly. Whether Judaism then, or western secularism today.

God providentially used the political experience of Felix to deliver Paul from Jewish hands (24.10). Although, Festus was a

179

novice (25.19), and a completely different character to Felix, God used his adherence to procedure to save Paul (25.5; cf. 25.16). After all, God can use anyone to accomplish his purpose. It would have been very easy to summon Paul to Jerusalem from Caesarea. Everyone was in place. Festus was looking to enhance diplomatic ties with the Jews (25.9) and Festus had at least another eight days at Jerusalem (25.6). Further, Festus initially thought the Jews had a case against Paul, 'assuming that there is anything amiss in this man' (25.5, Wuest, cf. 25.18). Humanly speaking, Paul should have gone to Jerusalem and been caught in the Jewish assassination trap but God, Who works all things after the counsel of his own will and directs the hearts of rulers as He pleases (Prov 21.1), used Festus' love of procedure to try Paul in the provincial capital of Caesarea. Paul had served his purpose in Jerusalem, and was not going back there - God was moving him onwards to Rome (23.11).

In Caesarea (vv6-12)

Considering it was Festus' first official visit to Jerusalem, Luke emphasises the brevity of his stay – 'not more than eight or ten days' (25.6, JND). The Acts narrative continues to move away from Jerusalem.

Festus promptly arrived at Caesarea, and the next day sat on the 'bema' and commanded Paul to be brought. As soon as the court was in session the Jews surrounded Paul like a pack of wolves. Any pretence of legal procedure evaporated. At least before Felix they had brought Tertullus, showing some legal propriety. But now they bombarded him with novel and exaggerated accusations. The Jews changed tact and whipped up an accusatory maelstrom (cf. 25.24). Paul, however, in this pressure cooker environment, did not budge from the truth. The result was the same; despite their strident lobbying, their claims were unprovable (25.7). Paul's defence is written in shorthand by Luke (25.8), showing that his strategy was the same as in his trial before Felix. Paul had not sinned against 'Jewish law in general, or the sanctity of the temple in particular'[17] (25.8). Although the previous accusations from the Jews implied rebellion against Caesar (24.5), this time round the accusation were explicit as Paul says, 'nor yet against Caesar' (25.8). The Jews were following their tactics from Gabbatha, where they set up the Lord Jesus as being against Caesar (Jn 19.12).

For all his efficiency and adherence to procedure, in 'desiring to ingratiate himself with the Jews' (25.9, Wuest, cf. 24.27), Festus showed that he would compromise judicial procedure for political capital. Although appearing more moral than Felix, they were the same at heart. At this point the stakes could not have been higher. Paul was on the brink of being tried in Jerusalem and accused of treason. Paul knew that a trial in Jerusalem was as good as a guilty verdict, and a death penalty. The Jews had run that ploy on Paul's master (Jn 19.12). However, as soon as Festus mentioned Jerusalem, Paul immediately responded, saying; 'I stand at Caesar's judgement seat' (25.10). Even though Festus knew that Paul had done nothing wrong (25.11), he had shown a hint of compromise for political expediency. And the man that proved unfaithful in a small matter at Caesarea would be unfaithful at Jerusalem (Lk 16.10). Paul knew that Pilate had buckled under Jewish pressure, and Festus would be no different. This is why he appealed to Rome.

Paul exemplified Christian conduct in addressing a ruler who had been ordained by God, his sin notwithstanding. He does not rail against Festus (Jude 1.9); neither is he pushed around. He was no anarchist, taking justice into his own hands. Neither was he a pacifist, allowing the law to be unjustly used against him (25.11). Paul directly aims at the conscience of Festus, saying, '[I have] done no wrong as thou very well knowest' (25.10). Submitting to every human institution (cf. 1 Pet 2.13), Paul was willing to die if he had broken the law. Every Christian should 'obey rule' (Titus 3.1, YLT), but if human legislation conflicts with divine righteousness, they ought to hold their ground, prepared to accept any consequences that follow; for better or worse (cf. 1 Pet 3.14). Ultimately, every Christian submits to the dealings of the Judge of all the earth to Whom vengeance belongs.

As soon as Paul lodged his formal appeal, Festus resumed form and followed procedure. He swiftly conferred with his own council (a body of men chosen by the governor himself from the principal Romans of the province[18]) and summarily announced, 'to Caesar shalt thou go' (25.12).

23

PAUL AND HEROD AGRIPPA II (25.13-26.22)

In Private (25.13-22)

Paul was destined to bear the name of Christ before kings (9.15). Agrippa ruled several provinces to the north-east of Festus and was the son of Herod Agrippa I[19] (12.1). He and his sister Bernice were aristocracy, and God in His grace saw fit to present the gospel to this debauched pair.[20]

Providentially they arrived at the right time, as Festus was unsure about the charges to send to Caesar (25.27), but Agrippa was an expert in Jewish affairs (26.3). Festus used this to his advantage since he had to send Paul's defence to Caesar. Paul had to 'show that the gospel ... was not a form of treason ... he was in a sense already addressing Caesar; for what he [was going to say] would form the basis of Festus' letter to the Emperor.'[21] Agrippa's visit started as a polite formality in visiting the new governor (25.13), but God would use it bring the gospel to Nero himself.

Festus had little regard for Paul and the gospel, viewing him only as 'a certain man left by Felix' (25.14), and his message as 'certain points ... about their own religion' (25.19, ESV). Paul's case was low on Festus' list of priorities; he was not discussed for 'many days' (25.14). 'The tone of Festus about Paul ... is certainly one of superficial ... indifference. Paul is one of Felix's leftovers (left behind), a sort of "junk" left on his hands.'[22] Just like a previous governor and Herod were made friends over a religious prisoner (Lk 23.12), history was repeating itself as their successors strengthened political ties over the apostle.

In private conversation with Agrippa, it became clear that Festus knew that the Jews wanted Paul dead. They sought 'a sentence of condemnation against [Paul]' (25.15, NASB), and wanted him delivered to death (25.16). Festus proudly narrates his adherence to Roman law (25.16) and has an air of superiority about him as he looks down his nose at the Jewish attempt to circumvent procedure. Pontificating about his own righteousness, as the arbiter of Roman justice, he sits on the *bema* (25.17). He glosses over his judicial compromise, benignly saying; 'I asked [Paul] whether he would go to Jerusalem' (25.20). Festus presented himself as a paragon of virtue to Agrippa, all the while preventing Paul's release. Felix was an obvious rogue, but Festus hid behind a veneer of morality. The Lord, however, knew his heart (cf. Rom 2.1).

Festus's secular indifference becomes evident when he speaks about the Lord Jesus as 'a certain Jesus' (25.19). He sees Paul as an inconvenient annoyance who 'kept on asserting [that Jesus] is alive' (25.19, Wuest). Devoted to Augustus (lit. the august one … a title of Roman emperors[23], cf. *kyrios*, 25.26), Festus thought little of Christ. His perplexity about Jewish matters (25.20, cf. 25.26-27) furnished Agrippa with an opportunity to hear Paul. This Herod, like Antipas before him (Lk 23.8), was eager to meet the leading men of 'the Way'. Festus, man of procedure as he was, jumped at the opportunity and turned an informal hearing into an occasion for formal charges to be sent to Rome.

In Court (25.23-27)

Since Paul had already appealed to Caesar, he was not bound by law to stand before Agrippa. He was willing, however, to become all things to all men to save some (1 Cor 9.22). Therefore, he patiently endures the egotistical fanfare of Agrippa and Festus (v23) and steps into the cauldron of scrutiny with the commanders of Caesarea (each a leader of a thousand … there were five cohorts of soldiers stationed in Caesarea[24]).

In this legal amphitheatre, Festus briefly outlines the case to his esteemed audience. He spins the account to distance himself from the case, saying that it was the Jews who had brought Paul before him (25.24), and made out that Paul had taken it upon himself to appeal to Caesar (instead of having his hand forced) (25.25). In a neat sleight of hand, he then passes Paul over to his audience saying, 'I have brought him forth before you, and specially before thee, O king Agrippa' (25.26). Like Pilate before him (Mt 27.24), he was washing his hands of this difficult case. His actions were not only unreasonable (25.27), but unjust.

The injustice of human courts can be perplexing until we realise that this has been foretold by the Bible: 'I saw under the sun the place of judgment, that wickedness was there; and the place of righteousness, that iniquity was there' (Ecc 3.16). Although this can be depressing, we must remember that God is the righteous Judge who will eventually right every wrong.

Commencement (26.1-3)

For the first time in all his trials Paul is not making a legal defence in a pressure cooker environment but has relative freedom to give his personal testimony. His boldness is admirable (26.26). He stretches out his hand to the ruling aristocracy; '[conveying] a trait descriptive of the solemnity of this moment: Paul comes forward in the attitude of an orator, with all the ingenuousness and candour of a good conscience'.[25] His chained hand (26.29) was lifted high for the 'hope of Israel' (28.20). This hope – a resurrected Messiah – could also be Agrippa's hope. Paul reflects the earnest pleading of his Lord: 'all day long I have stretched forth my hands' (Rom 10.21).

He proceeds to make an apologetic for himself (26.1) conscious that his suffering is a blessing (26.2): 'If ye suffer for righteousness' sake, [blessed] are ye: and be not afraid of their terror … but sanctify the Lord God in your hearts: and be ready always to give an [apologetic] … [for] the hope that is in you' (1 Pet 3.12-13).

God's providence was working again for Paul, as Agrippa was an expert in Jewish theology and practise (questions and customs, 26.3). Amongst the legal jousting of previous trials, it was difficult to give a longform explanation of the gospel. Without the Jews breathing down his neck, God had now opened 'a great door' (1 Cor 16.9) and Paul asked Agrippa to listen with endurance (26.3). The gospel message requires serious consideration and is not a 'catchy one liner'.

Curriculum Vitae (26.4-11)
Theology (vv4-8)

From his earliest days, Paul was a dyed-in-the-wool Jew. His pedigree was impeccable and known to all (26.4). Five definite articles 'give additional precision to the statement'[26] (26.4). He was a Pharisee of the Pharisees, adhering to 'the most precise and rigorous interpretation of Mosaic law.'[27] He was completely orthodox, believing in a future resurrection, and Messiah's Kingdom as Israel's hope. The Jews hoped to be raised to enter this Messianic Kingdom, but Paul knew that this hope could only be realised through acknowledging Jesus of Nazareth as Messiah and Lord. They hoped for the same thing but hoped in a different One. This was the heart of the contention all along. Was Jesus of Nazareth the fulfilment of Jewish hopes? The resurrection of Christ (23.6; 24.21; 25.19) was foundational to any Kingdom or Jewish blessing. Paul shows that the Jewish hope (26.6-7) was built upon the resurrection of Christ (26.8). The two could not be divorced. They went together, 'hand in glove'. If the Lord Jesus wasn't raised, there was no Kingdom and no resurrection for the Jews. They could have no Kingdom without Jesus Christ.

Agrippa and the Jews believed in the resurrection generally but would not admit the specific resurrection of the Lord Jesus. Even though it was public news in Jerusalem (26.26), they would not believe. Paul points out the incongruity of their position, asking the obvious rhetorical question: 'Why is it judged incredible with you, if God doth raise the dead? (26.8, YLT)'.

In showing his track record, Paul aligns himself with the Pharisees (26.5), the fathers (26.6), the twelve tribes (26.7), and the Jews generally (26.4, 7). They all ardently devoted themselves to this hope: 'our religion (reverent worship, not external ritual[28])', 'night and day rendering sacred service to God (26.5, Wuest). Three times over Paul proclaims this shared hope (26.6, 7), 'the promise made unto the fathers.' Despite believing the same thing, Paul points out the oddity of his current predicament. He was being accused and judged for this shared hope (26.6, 8).

Practise (vv9-11)

Paul has aligned himself with Jewish orthodoxy, and now shows his previous alignment with Jewish orthopraxy (cf. Gal 1.13-14; Phil 3.6; 1 Tim 1.15). He had started with the same ignorance and hatred for Jesus of Nazareth. He showed the severity with which he opposed the saints, imprisoning some and casting his voting stone[29] in favour of the execution of others (plural, 26.10). He threw this stone at Stephen. He showed the extent to which he was willing to pursue them, hunting them like animals to foreign lands (26.11). Two present participles (punishing and being mad), and two imperfect indicatives (kept on compelling and kept on persecuting), vividly portray the relentless hatred of Saul the Benjamite. 'He was true to type; "Benjamin shall ravin as a wolf".'[30] It was a work of grace that changed him to 'the beloved of the Lord ... who shelters him all the day long' (Deut 33.12, NKJV).

The first half of his defence has shown his alignment with the Jews. He is essentially saying 'I was one of you.' He will proceed to show how and why everything changed, and in so doing answer their charges (26.2). The man that was contrary to Jesus of Nazareth, was converted. He was the most unlikely and unwilling convert, the chief of sinners. But if Paul could come to realise that Jesus of Nazareth was the true and living hope of Israel, then any other Jew could believe as well. The irrefutable proof was that Jesus of Nazareth was alive and, therefore, Lord and God. Being the fulfilment of the Jewish hope, He had changed Paul's life forever. This was the only conclusion, and had eternal implications for everyone.

'Paul's testimony contains two main themes: Jesus Christ's resurrection proves Him to be the Messiah, and Paul's transformed life proves the reality of Christ's resurrection. He masterfully weaves the saving gospel through this first-person account'[31].

Paul's conversion testimony – a radically changed eyewitness of the resurrection – is a great apologetic for the gospel. In the work of evangelism, we can use the conversion of Paul, combined with our own testimony, as powerful witnesses. As the Lord said to the exorcised demoniac, 'Go ... to thy friends and tell them how great things the Lord hath done for thee, and hath had compassion on thee' (Mk 5.19).

Conversion (vv12-15)

Each time Luke records the Damascus Road experience, he does so with increasing intensity (cf. 9.3; 22.6; 26.13). Similarly, we should pray 'restore unto me the joy of my salvation' (Ps 51.12). Paul describes the *Shekinah* glory that engulfed him on his journey as brighter than the noon-day sun (26.13). His first mention of 'them which journeyed with me … were all fallen to the earth' (v13-14), showed that this was not his imagination.[32] By speaking in the Hebrew tongue (26.14), the Lord was showing that this was in line with Old Testament revelation. He was Jehovah, the covenant God of Israel, providing new revelation.[33] It must have been mind-blowing for Paul to hear Jehovah say 'I am Jesus' (26.15).

Commission (26.16-23)
Personal (vv16-18)
Paul now narrates the consequences of the Damascus Road experience. This section is full of commissioning language. The Lord is personally sending Paul, as He had the other apostles. Paul is given marching orders as two imperatives (rise and stand) call him to attention (26.16). He is to be an official minister (lit. an under-rower, subordinate to His commander) and witness (authoritative testifier) of past and future revelation (26.16). His apostleship was not of or by men, but by the risen Christ (Gal 1.1).

Three times in the overall commission the Gentiles are mentioned (26.17, 20, 23). Each time there is a primary Jewish emphasis. Although the Lord said 'to [the Gentiles] now I send (*apostellō*) thee' (26.17), Paul often went to the Jew first, then to the Gentiles. Given his current audience, this Gentile emphasis is fitting. The Lord pledged to appear again to Paul (26.16). He was a steward of the mysteries of God (1 Cor 4.1), mysteries belonging to a new dispensation. What he had learnt in embryonic form on the Damascus Road – that there was a persecuted body linked to a risen head (Who felt that persecution) – would be expanded later. He learnt that uniquely in the dispensation of grace, Jews and Gentiles are one new man in Christ. This was a new race of men, not an extension or replacement of Israel, but a brand-new entity, called the Church, the bride of Christ (Eph 2.14-3.7).

Jew and Gentile were both constituted saints and received equally a heavenly inheritance (26.18; cf. 1 Pet 1.4). Illumination, translation, remission, and participation in an inheritance was all part of his gospel message (26.18). 'Doubtless Jews needed these operations of grace no less than the nations; but in the latter case the necessity was far more conspicuous, besotted as they were in shameless immorality and gross superstitions which darkened and demoralized them.'[34] Paul not only rejoiced in his own salvation, but in that of others; elsewhere he thanks the Father that the largely Gentile audience in Colosse experienced exactly this (26.18, Col 1.11-14).

Public (vv19-23)

Like Peter the apostle to the Jews, Paul 'could not but speak of the things that he had seen and heard' (4.20). Disobedience was inconceivable (26.19). The 'heavenly vision' had the stamp of authenticity about it. Just as Ezekiel saw the heavens opened and visions of God (Eze 1.1) prior to his commission (Eze 2.1-3), Paul had received a divine message from Jehovah Himself. This was binding for every Jew and Gentile. Just as the Lord went about all the cities and villages preaching (Mt 9.35), Paul did the same (26.20). He started locally in Damascus, and then covered thousands of miles (26.20). With a sense of compulsion to pay off this 'gospel-debt', he was unashamed to preach to Jews and Gentiles (Rom 1.14-16). He felt constrained to preach, exclaiming 'woe is unto me if I preach not the gospel!' (1 Cor 9.16). He dared not squander the grace of God bestowed upon him, labouring more than all others (1 Cor 15.10). In a day of sickening lukewarmness, may we follow his example.

Paul preached justification by faith for salvation and justification by works (James 2.21) – 'works meet for repentance' (26.20). Works never precede, but always following saving faith. If there is no fruit, there is no life (Mt 7.20).

Paul makes clear that the Jews tried to kill him (26.21), not for treason or temple desecration, but for preaching the gospel to the Gentiles. Gentile blessing was an anathema to the Jews. Notwithstanding the murderous intentions of the Jews (26.21), Paul pressed on. This again, was evidence of the resurrection. Even though his outward man was threatened and perishing the inner man was experiencing the daily power of resurrection (2 Cor 4.16). The Jewish zealot who persecuted Christians, now under threat of death preached with greater zeal the gospel of Christ. The only reasonable explanation for this was that Jesus of Nazareth was the Son of God, alive from the dead. Despite the murder plots, God was Paul's constant ally (help, 26.22). His message was in perfect harmony with Moses and the prophets, as Agrippa well knew (26.27). His message was the fulfilment of Jewish expectation, and light to the Gentiles (26.23; cf. Is 42.6; 49.6). Christ was the first in rank from the dead (Col 1.18), and Paul was not only making a defence of his message but offering this Saviour to the royal audience.

Conclusion (26.24-32)

Festus was a natural man and saw the resurrection as madness (26.24, cf. 1 Cor 2.14). Paul however was not afraid of the foolishness of preaching (1 Cor 1.21) but calmly responded to Festus' outburst. Showing the coherence of his message, Paul appealed to Agrippa's mind (26.26). The king had abundant evidence that Christ was risen (26.27), but 'how little such acquaintance with facts avails unless the Holy Spirit bring the word of God home to an exercised conscience.'[35] As he had done with Felix (24.24) and the small and great he had encountered (26.22), Paul applied the gospel personally to Agrippa (26.27).

Although Agrippa knew the truth he deflected the appeal by saying '(lit.) in a little thou persuadest me to become a Christian' (26.28, Darby). Words of levity are often used to try and avoid the solemn gospel message. Whether in a little time, labour, or speech,[36] Paul had done his utmost to persuade Agrippa and discharged his responsibility. Exuding truth and grace, Paul replied that 'whether by much or by little persuasion' (26.29, Wuest), he wanted them to be saved.

Behind closed doors the unanimous verdict was 'this man doeth nothing worthy of death or bonds' (26.31). He followed his Lord – a 'just man' (Mt 27.19) who had done 'nothing amiss' (Lk 23.41).

24

THE ROUTE TO ROME (27-28)

Paul's long-term prayer to visit Rome (19.21; Rom 1.9-12) was answered (28.16), although perhaps not as he imagined. Following his arrest in Jerusalem, subsequent trials (21.31-26.32), and appeal to Caesar (25.11), he left for Rome as a prisoner. On the way he endured shipwreck (27.1-44) and three months on Malta as a castaway (28.1-10), before finally arriving in Rome (28.11-16). Despite being under a form of house arrest, Paul was able to serve the Lord for two years in Rome (28.16-31).

Shipwreck (27.1-44)

Luke's account is gripping because it is first-hand ('we', vv1, 2, 3, 4, 5, 7, 15, 16, 18, 19, 20, 27, 37). He captures the tension between Paul and the ship's pilot over the decision to sail (vv4, 7, 9-12), the apparent vindication of the pilot (v13) before the sudden arrival of the storm (v14), and the ensuing loss of all hope on the ship (v20). Remarkably, at this point Paul, the prisoner, assumed control of the situation (v21), orchestrating an improbable but successful rescue (v44, cf. Ps 107.23-32). This passage dispels the myth that to be heavenly minded makes one of no earthly use.

Paul was entrusted to Julius, a **courteous centurion (vv1-5)**, and one of Augustus Caesar's guards (v1). He was an effective organiser (v6), unafraid of consultation (vv11-12), and yet able to authoritatively command his men (vv42, 43). Although he was responsible for several prisoners (v1), Luke notes that he treated Paul 'courteously' (v3, *philanthrōpōs*, loving mankind). In the NT centurions are consistently referenced in praiseworthy terms, and Julius is no exception. Like Joseph (Gen 39.21), and Daniel (Dan 1.9), God brought Paul into *favour* with the person responsible for him. At their first port, Sidon, Julius allowed Paul to refresh himself with *friends*. The same people that Paul once persecuted on his travels had become a network of friends (cf. arriving in Rome, 28.14, 15, 30). In addition, God provided *fellowship* onboard the ship in the presence of Luke, 'the beloved physician' (Col 4.14), and Aristarchus, his 'fellow labourer' and 'fellow prisoner' (v2; cf. 19.29; 20.4; Col 4.10; Phm 24). Together, these tokens of mercy surely made the bitter pill of lost liberty easier for Paul to swallow.

The 'ship of Adramyttium'(v2), or modern-day Turkey, that carried them from Caesarea intended to hug the coast to Macedonia, perhaps explaining why Aristarchus of Macedonia was on board. At Myra however, Julius arranged passage on 'a ship of Alexandria', an Egyptian city, destined for Italy (v6). Following a meandering route (v7), the ship continued its slow land-hugging course before arriving at the Fair Havens, a port on the south side of the island of Crete (v8). Despite its name, it was not a good place to winter (v12), and this became the source of **friction at the Fair Havens (vv6-12)**. Paul's advice was not to sail. Luke gives no indication that special revelation informed Paul's counsel. In fact, the special revelation he did have at this point affirmed that he would get to Rome (23.11). But Paul did not take this knowledge to mean normal precautions were now unnecessary, and accordingly, his advice was based on experience and plain common sense: given the time of year, embarking on a voyage was dangerous (v9). Paul had suffered multiple shipwrecks (2 Cor 11.25) and clearly had no appetite to go through it unnecessarily. But Paul's voice was drowned out by the cumulative forces of *expert advice* – 'the master and owner of the ship' (v11); *majority opinion* – 'the more part advised to depart' (v12);

and *calculated risk* – 'if by any means they might attain to Phenice, and there to winter' (v12). Sailing to Phenice, a safer wintering port a short distance along the coast of Crete, was not a big risk to take, surely? But as it transpired, 'the man who knew God was wiser than the men who knew the sea'[37]. Our best plans are those made in close consultation with the throne of grace (Pr 3.6).

The *power of nature* is illustrated by **the storm at sea (vv13-20)**. Man's creative ability to usefully harness wind and water sets him above the animal kingdom. It is part of the dignity of being made in the image of God, and in harmony with the original mandate to exercise dominion over the earth (Gen 1.26-28; Ps 8.3-8). Man can design sailing vessels, navigate making intelligent use of the stars (v20), and develop strategies for weathering storms (vv15-17). But there is a point at which the forces of nature are overwhelming, and we must say, 'Thou rulest the raging of the sea' (Ps 89.9) and take refuge in the omnipotent God Himself. Man is not the captain of his own destiny, far less the planet's. The 'helps' with which they undergirded the ship, involved passing ropes around the hull and tying them together to provide additional reinforcement for the storm. The same word is taken up by the Hebrew writer to encourage us to the throne of grace, that me might find 'grace to help in time of need' (Heb 4.16). Divinely supplied reinforcement is constantly available to hold us together in the storms of life.

The move to lighten the ship reveals the intrinsic *preciousness of life*. Discarding weight raised the ship's level in the water, reducing the risk of waves swamping the boat. First to go was the cargo (v18). Next, after three days, was the tackling. This was evidently heavy, requiring the help of all onboard to jettison (v19). Understandably at this point they kept their food (v36); this was necessary to sustain life. But notice they did not throw the prisoners overboard. Later the soldiers considered killing them, for a Roman soldier could forfeit his life if he lost his prisoner (v42, cf. 12.19), but in the storm, their subconscious value system evidently placed a higher significance on preserving the life of all on board, prisoners included, than on possessions and potential profit. Life is intrinsically precious precisely because we are made 'in the image of God' (Gen 1.27; Gen 9.6), and this knowledge is stamped on the heart of man (Rom 2.14-15), explaining why we instinctively want to rescue people in danger and cure sick people.

The direct assurance Paul had already received from the Lord Himself, that he would arrive in Rome and stand before Caesar (23.11), was complemented by **the Angel's announcement (vv21-26).** The supplementary information given by the angel of God included specific promises: there would be no loss of life; the ship would be lost; they would be cast on a certain island. This is an example of *special revelation* received by Paul direct from God (cf. 1 Cor 11.23; 15.3; Gal 1.12). Today we have the word of God, completed by the apostles as pre-authenticated by Christ (Jn 14.26). It forms the only authoritative source of information about Christ, through Whom we have 'all things that *pertain* unto life and godliness' (2 Pet 1.3). We cannot therefore expect additional revelation. Instead, for all our needs we rely on God, and His inspired, infallible word (20.32; 1 Cor 13.8-10; Jude 3; Rev 22.18).

The self-validating prophetic utterances provided *solace* to Paul. His glad and bold identification with God - 'whose I am, and whom I serve' (v23), is the exemplary response of a soul enabled to cheerfully endure suffering in the confident expectation of coming glory. The word from the Lord also acted as a *summons* to the centurion, pilot, and shipmen to place their faith in the Lord; for it bore all the hallmarks of a practical demonstration that God's word is completely reliable (cf. Jn 14.29; Is 48.5). Paul demonstrated the sublime simplicity of what it means to believe, stating: 'I believe

God, that it shall be even as it was told me' (v25). The God who cannot lie will unfailingly bring His word to pass, and faith acts on that unreservedly. If Paul's shipmates responded like Jonah's, by calling on the Lord (cf. Jonah 1.16), then we will see them in heaven.

There is 'a time to keep silence, and a time to speak' (Ecc 3.7); and Paul judged both just right. Resisting the temptation to say, 'I told you so', Paul spoke only 'after long abstinence' (v21), for he was characterized by *self-control*. The adage: 'if you've nothing helpful to say, say nothing' is correct; but when Paul had something helpful from the Lord to say, he promptly spoke up.

With the ship fast approaching land in the dead of night, pretending to cast an anchor from the front of the ship, **the sneaky shipmen (vv27-32)** were in fact letting down a boat for themselves to escape in. Paul, ever a *vigilant* leader, and no doubt aided by his thorough understanding of the sin nature, spotted their deception (20.31, cf.1 Cor 16.13; Col 4.2), and acting in harmony with the revealed will of God, gave *decisive* instruction that they must stay with the ship. Paul's word was *authoritative,* for the soldiers promptly cut the boat loose, leaving the sailors with the ship. His authority came from having God's word and speaking it boldly.

Four anchors were dropped from the ship's stern, providing a resilient, unseen, connection for the storm-tossed ship to the security of the ocean bed below; giving hope of safety when otherwise they would be dashed on the rocks (v29). The Hebrew writer applies this imagery to the hope set before us in the gospel: 'which hope we have as an anchor of the soul, both sure and stedfast, and which entereth into that within the veil; whither the forerunner is for us entered, even Jesus' (Heb 6.19, 20). Our anchor is our hope, and our hope is Christ (1 Tim 1.1). He is located not on the seabed below, but high above us, 'inside the veil', in the very presence of God which he has 'for us entered' (Heb 6.20). We are securely connected to Him not by four ropes, but by His unbreakable word of promise, doubly confirmed by an oath for our reassurance (Heb 6.17,18). Anchored to Christ, the storms may toss our soul like the ship at sea, but we are inseparably connected to Christ, and eternally secure (Rom 8.39).

Paul's leadership again emerges at **the big breakfast (vv33-38);** big, because it was the first meal all 266 souls had had in fourteen days. His authority was now well established, but wherever possible he preferred the winsome approach, meaning he 'besought' rather than commanded the people to eat (cf. Philem 8, 9). His appeal to eat for their wellbeing (v34) shows faith in God's revealed word going hand in hand with responsible action: Paul recognised they needed a meal to give them the physical strength to get to a 'certain island' after the ship was lost (vv22, 26). Paul's leadership was exemplary, as he ate in front of those on the ship (v35), which encouraged them to do likewise (v36). He further set an example by giving thanks to God before eating (v35), imitating the pattern set by Christ (e.g., Mt 15.36), and laying down a right habit for us to follow today. Supplementing his example Paul used encouragement, reassuring those on the ship with the Christlike phrase, 'there shall not an hair fall from the head of any of you' (v34; cf. Lk 21.18). Those who have experienced divine comfort are best placed to offer it to others (cf. 2 Cor 1.3-4)

In accordance with the divine promise, all were **saved from the shipwreck (vv39-44).** An apparent threat arose to the fulfilment of God's word when the soldiers decided to kill the prisoners (v42). But God, who 'worketh all things after the counsel of His own will' (Eph 1.11), used the Centurion's good will toward Paul to uphold His word, and Julius stopped his men for the sake of Paul. Upon running the ship aground, its 'forepart stuck fast, and remained unmoveable', while its 'hinderpart was broken with the violence of the waves' (v41). The Hebrew writer takes up the imagery, describing the kingdom which we are receiving as 'unmoveable'. Applying the thought, we are either pouring our efforts into things that will stand firm, or that will be washed away (2 Cor 4.18). Accordingly, Paul encouraged the Corinthians: 'my beloved brethren, be ye stedfast, unmoveable, always abounding in the work of the Lord, forasmuch as ye know that your labour is not in vain in the Lord' (1 Cor 15.58).

Three months in Malta (28.1-11)

The original voyage from Crete was intended to take them to a near port, but it ended on Malta, the best part of 1,000km away, giving force to the analogy drawn by Paul between the horrors of shipwreck and the effect of abandoning faith and a good conscience (cf. 1 Tim 1.19). The moment we override our conscience, or the word of God, we may begin a chain reaction that leads us dangerously off course.

In Malta, the shipwreck survivors met the non-Greek speaking inhabitants, or 'barbarous people', (v2) who proved **merciful**: all 266 survivors were welcomed and warmed at their fire. Luke described their actions as kindness (v2, *philanthrōpía*) similar to Julius' courtesy (27.3, *philanthrōpōs*). As well as illustrating the marvellous providence of God, this episode provides important biblical evidence in relation to the doctrine of man's sinfulness. When the Bible concludes that we are 'all under sin' (Rom 3.9), it evidently doesn't mean that unregenerate man is incapable of anything positive, as the philanthropy of these yet un-evangelised islanders shows. For many, the hardest aspect of man's sinfulness to accept is that even our best moments fall short of the glory of God (Rom 3.23, Is 64.6).

When Paul was attacked by a viper from the fire, their **moral** framework emerged. They assumed he was a murderer and expected him shortly to fall down dead in recompense for his past crime. The executor of 'vengeance' is not named, the justness of a murderer forfeiting his life was not questioned; it seems they had observed and accepted a sowing and reaping principle in life, although they were ignorant of the God who works it out (Gal 6.7). Their instinctive response is an example of what Paul described as the 'work of the law written in their hearts' (Rom 2.15). God has engraved a working knowledge of righteousness on man's heart, and we may use this knowledge to appeal to people's consciences when evangelising.

No sooner had Paul shaken the viper from his arm, than the Maltese people change their mind, concluding he was a god (v6)! Without the light of written revelation man is **muddled**; creation and conscience make man accountable (Rom 1.20), but do not provide a complete disclosure of God and His ways. Unless the believer is built up by the word of God we too will be 'tossed to and fro and carried about with every wind of doctrine' (Eph 4.14).

The islanders became **miracle-beneficiaries**: for they saw Paul unharmed by the viper – one of the specific signs the Lord foretold would accompany the preaching of the gospel (Mk 16.18). Along with the healing of Publius' father (v8) and widespread healings of diseased islanders (v9), the apostolic miracles were special signs empowered by God to validate their witness to the resurrection (1.22, Mk 16.20, Heb 2.4). It is reasonable to therefore assume Paul preached the gospel to these people. By what unexpected means the Lord of the harvest brings the evangelist and hearer together at times (Lk 10.2)! The Islanders, understandably, wanted to honour them on their departure. Their generosity and discretion are combined in Luke's summary: 'they laded us with such things as were necessary' (v10).

Finally arriving in Rome (28.11-16)
Leaving Malta by ship they hugged the south-west coast of Italy, prior to landing at Puteoli, and travelling to Rome by land. Luke

noticed the **ship's sign**: 'Castor and Pollux', twins from Greek mythology who were represented on the vessel (v11). The pair were regarded as the 'gods of mariners, to whom all their good fortune was ascribed'.[38] The contrast between such superstitions and the true God who rules the waves stands out. Paul's appeal to those of Lystra is apt here; '(we) preach unto you that ye should turn from these vanities unto the living God, which made heaven, and earth, and the sea, and all things that are therein' (14.15).

A **search for saints** occurred in Puteoli where they 'found brethren'. They largeheartedly accommodated the group, presumably including the soldiers and prisoners, 'seven days' (v14). This would have provided the opportunity to break bread (cf. 20.7). Accommodating such a stop may suggest that Julius was sympathetic to the gospel. It also points to the spread of the gospel, for wherever Paul went, there were pockets of saints to be found; and Paul searched them out. News of their approach went before them, and a welcoming party from Rome came to meet them. As a result, Paul 'thanked God, and took courage', underlining that there is nothing to substitute an in-person visit (cf. 2 Jn 1.12). The word 'meet' (*apántēsis*) expresses a loving welcome given to an arriving friend and is used by Paul to describe the moment when we will 'meet' the Lord in the air at His return for the church (1 Thess 4:17). We will forever thank God for that meeting.

At Rome the prisoners were delivered to 'the captain of the guard', but Paul was placed under house arrest, and one **set-apart soldier** was given the responsibility of guarding him (v16). Think of all he heard. Paul was also a set-apart soldier, and his preferential treatment was no mistake, it was the sovereign overruling of God, which meant, even though in bonds, he was free to engage in spiritual warfare (Eph 6.11-18).

Two years in Rome (28.17-31)

True to his habit, Paul sought a Jewish audience first in his new location, calling 'the chief of the Jews together' (v17). His first purpose was to provide an **explanation** for his imprisonment. Having appealed to Caesar, it was important to establish that he was not a criminal, nor set against his nation (v19); after all, a justly incarcerated, disloyal, evangelist is hardly a good advert for the message. Paul used the occasion to win a further hearing, referring to the 'hope of Israel' (v20) as the reason for his chain. There is an inextricable link between the gospel and Israel's future, for Christ is at the centre of both (cf. Rom 9-11). The response of the Roman Jews shows that, although they had heard nothing specific of Paul (v21), they had certainly heard derogatory reports about 'the way' he represented (v22).

Like Esther, Paul did not try to say everything on the first occasion (cf. Esther 5.3, 6, 8), but sought successive audiences which gave the opportunity for **exposition** (v23). When the word of God is being set forth in order, it is an ideal scenario to invite people to hear something of the breadth of God's truth. Paul's subject was 'the kingdom of God', that great programme of God's which embraces both His purpose for the nation of Israel and the church; his strategy was to 'persuade them concerning Jesus'; his source, 'the law of Moses, and…the prophets' for the apostolic gospel involved proving from the scriptures that Jesus is the Christ (cf. 17.2-3). His seriousness is seen from the fact that he spoke 'from morning till evening' (v23). This was not a hobby. It was his life.

The **ending** of Luke's record of Paul's ministry is striking, because after two years in Rome (v30) we are left to wonder, what happened next? Luke concludes by summarising the two responses to Paul's presentation of Christ in Rome: 'some believed the things which were spoken, and some believed not' (v24, cf. 17.32). There was reception and rejection. This encourages evangelism, but with realistic expectations. To the rejectors, Paul pressed home their solemn accountability with a rebuke taken from Isaiah (cf. Isa 6.9-10): 'their eyes they have closed' (v27). Israel's general and wilful rejection of God's Son was the divinely designed catalyst for salvation to be offered beyond Israel to the Gentiles (v28; cf. Rom 11.11). It is significant therefore that Acts, which began in Jerusalem with the gospel offered first to the Jews, ends in Rome with it going out to the Gentiles.

Paul's circumstances could hardly be described as ideal but look what God can accomplish in non-ideal circumstances. Perhaps we too can identify some improvement to our liberty, or opportunity, or ability, that we think would allow us to do something for God. Let each difficulty remind us of God's ways with Paul, who came to realise that his weakness was his strength – for God deposits His treasure in 'earthen vessels, that the excellency of the power may be of God, and not of us' (2 Cor 4.7).

NOTES

INTRODUCTION

[1]Jensen IL. *Jensen's Survey of the New Testament* (Chicago: Moody Press, 1981), p. 219.

[2]Bruce FF. *The Book of the Acts* (Grand Rapids, Michigan: Wm. B Eerdmans Publishing Company, Reprinted 1984), p. 368.

[3]Ibid., p. 375.

[4]Ibid., p. 474.

[5]Ibid., p. 26.

[6]Ibid., p. 255.

PART 1. JERUSALEM, JUDAEA, AND SAMARIA (1.1-8.25)

[1]Vine WE. *Expository Dictionary of New Testament Words* (Massachusetts: Hendrickson Publishers), p. 98.

[2]*Vincent's Word Studies of the New Testament*, 4 vols. (Hendrickson Publishers), vol. 1, p. 455.

[3]*Vincent's Word Studies of the New Testament*, 4 vols. (Hendrickson Publishers), vol. 1, p. 462.

[4]Ibid., p. 463.

[5]Ibid., p. 463.

[6]Gooding D. *True to the Faith* (Coleraine, N Ireland: The Myrtlefield Trust, Reprinted 2013), pp. 97, 98.

[7]*WUEST'S EXPANDED TRANSLATION OF THE GREEK NEW TESTAMENT.*

[8]Bengel JA. *New Testament word studies* (Grand Rapids, Michigan: Kregel Publications, 1971), vol. 1, pp. 785, 786.

[9]Gooding D. *True to the Faith* (Coleraine, N Ireland: The Myrtlefield Trust, Reprinted 2013), p. 118.

[10]Constable TL. Notes on Acts, p. 173. Available: https://planobiblechapel.org/tcon/notes/pdf/acts.pdf

[11]Riddle JM. The Acts of the Apostles (Kilmarnock, Scotland: John Ritchie Ltd., 2012), p. 123.

[12]Wuest KS. *Word Studies in the Greek New Testament*, 4 vols. (Grand Rapids, Michigan: Eerdmans Publishing Company, 1970), Vol. 4, p. 291.

[13]Gaebelein AC. *The Acts of the Apostles* (Neptune, New Jersey: Loizeaux Brothers, Inc., 1961), p. 156.

PART 2. UNTO THE UTTERMOST PART OF THE EARTH (9.1-21.17)

[1]Ibid, p. 207.

[2]Marshall IH. *ACTS.* (Leicester, England: Inter-Varsity Press, Reprinted 1984), p. 201.

[3]*Davis Dictionary of the Bible* (London: Pickering & Inglis Ltd.), p. 162.

[4]Gooding D. *True to the Faith* (Coleraine, N Ireland: The Myrtlefield Trust, Reprinted 2013), p. 220.

[5]Marshall IH. *ACTS.* (Leicester, England: Inter-Varsity Press, Reprinted 1984), p. 202.

[6]Bruce FF. *The Book of the Acts* (Grand Rapids, Michigan: Wm. B Eerdmans Publishing Company, Reprinted 1984), pp. 207, 208.

[7]*Vincent's Word Studies of the New Testament*, 4 vols. (Hendrickson Publishers), vol. 1, p. 497.

[8]Ibid., p. 499.

[9]Gooding D. *True to the Faith* (Coleraine, N Ireland: The Myrtlefield Trust, Reprinted 2013), p. 213.

[10]*Robertson's Word Pictures*, cited in e-Sword.

[11]*Baker Encyclopedia of Bible Places* (Inter-Varsity Press, 1995), p. 96.

[12]Bruce FF. The Book of the Acts (Grand Rapids, Michigan: Wm. B Eerdmans Publishing Company, Reprinted 1984), p. 263.

[13]Ibid., p. 264.

[14]Vine WE. *Expository Dictionary of New Testament Words* (Massachusetts: Hendrickson Publishers), p. 862.

[15]Pisidian Antioch | All About Turkey

[16]Gill DWJ, Gempf C. *The Book of Acts in its First Century Setting. Vol. 2: Graeco-Roman Setting* (Grand Rapids, Michigan: Wm. B Eerdmans Publishing Company, 1994), p. 384.

[17]Anstey, M. *Chronology of the Old Testament* (Kregel Publications, Grand Rapids, 1973, pp. 242, 243.

[18]Harris RL, Archer GL, Waltke BK. *Theological Wordbook of the Old Testament* (Chicago: Moody Publishers, 1980), p. 379.

[19]Phillips J. *Exploring Galatians (*Grand Rapids, Michigan: Kregel Publications, 2004), p. 68.

[20]Gill DWJ, Gempf C. *The Book of Acts in its First Century Setting. Vol. 2: Graeco-Roman Setting* (Grand Rapids, Michigan: Wm. B Eerdmans Publishing Company, 1994), p. 82.

[21]Gaebelein AC. *The Acts of the Apostles* (Neptune, New Jersey: Loizeaux Brothers, Inc., 1961), p. 253.

[22]Cambridge Greek Testament. *The Acts of the Apostles* (Cambridge: at the University Press, 1920), p. 269.

[23]Ibid, p. 282.

[24]*Baker Encyclopaedia of Bible Places* (Inter-Varsity Press, 1995), p. 92.

[25]Horner BE. *Future Israel: Why Christian Anti-Judaism Must Be Challenged* (Nashville, Tennessee: B&H Academic), p. 24.

[26]Ibid., p. 26.

[27]Ibid., p. 26.

[28]Conybeare WJ & Howson JS. *The Life and Epistles of St. Paul* (Grand Rapids, Michigan: Wm. B Eerdmans Publishing Company Reprinted 1992), p. 297.

[29]Vine WE. *Expository Dictionary of New Testament Words* (Massachusetts: Hendrickson Publishers), p. 934.

[30]Irvin A Busenitz in Macarthur JF. *Rediscovering Pastoral Ministry* (Dallas: Word Publishing, 1995), p. 129.

[31]Freeman P. *ALEXANDER THE GREAT* (New York, NY 10020: Simon & Schuster Paperbacks, 2011), pp. 87, 88.

[32]Calvin J. *Commentaries on the Epistle of Paul the Apostle to the Romans* (Christian Classics Ethereal Library, Grand Rapids, Michigan, Translated and Edited by John Owen), p. 13.

[33]Some make v11 refer to the Lord's supper (William Macdonald, FF Bruce), taking the phrase, 'broken bread and eaten' to contain two acts (the Lord's supper and a common meal). But 'eaten' (*'geúō'*, v11) is not used elsewhere in the NT in relation to the Lord's supper; and 'break bread' (v7) or 'broken bread' (v11) literally describes dividing food into portions to eat, either during a common meal (cf. Mt 14.19), or the Lord's supper (cf. Mt 26.26). It is better to take v7 as the observation of the Lord's supper, and v11 as participating in a common meal. Acts 2.42, 46 is another instance where the Lord's supper and a common meal are in similar proximity. Paul was habitually courteous – indeed, while in Troas, he was in a rush to Jerusalem, but rather than calling a special meeting to suit himself, he fitted in with their normal meeting time. He also taught that all things should be done 'decently and in order' (1 Cor 14.40). Therefore, it seems unlikely that he would allow his preaching to displace the act of remembrance to the second day of the week (v11 is after midnight), rather than occurring on the intended, and significant, first day of the week.

[34]*WUEST'S EXPANDED TRANSLATION OF THE GREEK NEW TESTAMENT.*

PART 3. PAUL'S ARREST, IMPRISONMENT, AND JOURNEY TO ROME (21.17-28.31)

[1]Bruce FF. *The Book of the Acts* (Grand Rapids, Michigan: Wm. B Eerdmans Publishing Company, Reprinted 1984), p. 436.

[2]Ibid, p. 445.

[3]Josephus, cited by Bruce FF. *The Book of the Acts* (Grand Rapids, Michigan: Wm. B Eerdmans Publishing Company, Reprinted 1984), p. 449.

[4]Marshall IH. *ACTS.* (Leicester, England: Inter-Varsity Press, Reprinted 1984), p. 362.

[5]Phillips J. *EXPLORING ACTS* (Neptune, New Jersey: Loizeaux Brothers, Inc., 1991), p. 442.

[6]FELIX (ANTONIUS FELIX) - JewishEncyclopedia.com

[7]Ibid.

[8]Robertson AT. *New Testament Word Pictures* on Acts 24.5.

[9]William Barclay, cited in Constable TL. *Notes on the Acts*, p. 463. Available at: Microsoft Word - Acts Notes 22.docx (planobiblechapel.org)

[10]Constable TL. *Notes on the Acts*, p. 463.

[11]Heinrich Meyer, cited in *Vincent's Word Studies of the New Testament*, 4 vols. (Hendrickson Publishers), vol. 1, p. 492.

[12]Richard Longenecker, cited by Constable TL. *Notes on the Acts*, p. 466.

[13]Bruce FF. *The Book of the Acts* (Grand Rapids, Michigan: Wm. B Eerdmans Publishing Company, Reprinted 1984), p. 472.

[14]Robertson AT. *New Testament Word Pictures* on Acts 25.1.

[15]Josephus: Antiquities of the Jews, Book XX (uchicago.edu) (chapter 8.9).

[16]Constable TL. *Notes on the Acts*, p. 471.

[17]Bruce FF. *The Book of the Acts* (Grand Rapids, Michigan: Wm. B Eerdmans Publishing Company, Reprinted 1984), p. 477.

[18]Vincent's Word Studies of the New Testament, 4 vols. (Hendrickson Publishers), Acts 25.12.

[19]Bruce FF. *The Book of the Acts* (Grand Rapids, Michigan: Wm. B Eerdmans Publishing Company, Reprinted 1984), p. 481.

[20]Chapter 5.3 Josephus: Antiquities of the Jews, Book XX (uchicago.edu)

[21]Gooding D. *True to the Faith* (Coleraine, N Ireland: The Myrtlefield Trust, Reprinted 2013), p. 359.

[22]Robertson AT. *New Testament Word Pictures* on Acts 25.14.

[23]*Vincent's Word Studies of the New Testament*, 4 vols. (Hendrickson Publishers), vol. 1, p. 586.

[24]Robertson AT. New Testament Word Pictures on Acts 25.23.

[25]*Meyer's Critical and Exegetical Commentary on the New Testament*, Acts 26.1. Available at: Acts 26 Meyer's NT Commentary (biblehub.com)

[26]*Vincent's Word Studies of the New Testament*, 4 vols. (Hendrickson Publishers), vol. 1, p. 586.

[27]*Thayer's Greek-English Lexicon of the New Testament*. Available at: G196 - akribēs - Strong's Greek Lexicon (kjv) (blueletterbible.org)

[28]Robertson AT. *New Testament Word Pictures* on Acts 26.4.

[29]Robertson AT. *New Testament Word Pictures* on Acts 26.10.

[30]Riddle JM. *The Acts of the Apostles* (Kilmarnock, Scotland: John Ritchie Ltd., 2012), pp. 379-380.

[31]MacArthur J. *The MacArthur New Testament Commentary – Acts 13-28* (Chicago, IL: Moody Publishers., 1996), pp. 332-333.

[32]Constable TL. *Notes on the Acts*, p. 479.

[33]Constable TL. *Notes on the Acts*, pp. 479–480.

[34]Kelly W. *An Exposition of the Acts of the Apostles – 3rd Edition* (London, C.A. Hammond, 1952), p. 373.

[35]Kelly W. *An Exposition of the Acts of the Apostles – 3rd Edition* (London, C.A. Hammond, 1952), p. 376.

[36]*Ellicott's Commentary for English Readers* – Acts 26.38. Available at: Acts 26 Ellicott's Commentary for English Readers (biblehub.com)

[37]Meyer FB. *Through the Bible Day by Day, A Devotional Commentary.* Accessed via E-sword.

[38]*Robertson's Word Pictures.* Accessed via E-Sword.